MW00825080

Divino Compañero

Princeton Theological Monograph Series

Recent volumes in the series:

Jeff B. Pool
*God's Wounds: Hermeneutic of the Christian Symbol
of Divine Suffering, Volume Two: Evil and Divine Suffering*

David H. Nikkel
Radical Embodiment

William J. Meyer
*Metaphysics and the Future of Theology:
The Voice of Theology in Public Life*

Myk Habets
The Anointed Son: A Trinitarian Spirit Christology

L. Paul Jensen
*Subversive Spirituality: Transforming Mission
through the Collapse of Space and Time*

Ilsup Ahn
*Position and Responsibility: Jürgen Habermas, Reinhold Niebuhr,
and the Co-Reconstruction of the Positional Imperative*

Eliseo Pérez-Álvarez
A Vexing Gadfly: The Late Kierkegaard on Economic Matters

Gale Heide
System and Story: Narrative Critique and Construction in Theology

Linda D. Peacore
The Role of Women's Experience in Feminist Theologies of Atonement

Divino Compañero

Toward a Hispanic Pentecostal Christology

Sammy Alfaro

PICKWICK *Publications* · Eugene, Oregon

DIVINO COMPAÑERO
Toward a Hispanic Pentecostal Christology

Princeton Theological Monograph Series 147

Pickwick Publications
An Imprint of Wipf and Stock Publishers
199 W. 8th Ave., Suite 3
Eugene, OR 97401

www.wipfandstock.com

ISBN 13: 978-1-60608-699-5

Cataloging-in-Publication data

Alfaro, Sammy G.

    Divino compañero : toward a Hispanic Pentecostal Christology / Sammy G.
Alfaro.

    Princeton Theological Monograph Series 147

    xii + 164 p. ; 23 cm. — Includes bibliographical references.

    ISBN 13: 978-1-60608-699-5

    1. Jesus Christ—Person and offices. 2. Hispanic American theology. 3. Hispanic
American Pentecostals. I. Title. II. Series.

BR1644 .A45 2010

Manufactured in the U.S.A.

To Miriam,

Thank you for accompanying me
throughout my academic pilgrimage.
I could not have accomplished this without you.

Contents

Acknowledgments

THE SUCCESSFUL COMPLETION OF A PHD DISSERTATION AND ITS EVENtual publication as a monograph has often been referred to as a rite of passage that permits the doctoral candidate to be inducted into the academy. As such, it reflects the effort of an individual and fails to pay homage to the community that pushed, tugged, and pulled to get the candidate through the gates. Looking back at my academic pilgrimage, I am reminded of the many individuals and institutions that helped me in one way or another to start, continue, and finish this journey. It would be impossible to acknowledge everyone here by name, so I will mention some groups in general and mention by name those people who assisted me in a special way and serve as representatives of the rest of one of these groups.

First of all, I am indebted to the Hispanic Pentecostal congregations, institutions, pastors, and scholars who have nurtured my Pentecostal faith and provided a foundational worldview that informs and inspires my theological endeavors. Among these I hold in high esteem my first pastor, Mario Ruiz Valenzuela, who urged me to attend the Bible Institute and ignited the spark for further academic achievement. My years at the "Iglesia de Dios en Glendale" were formative in my biblical and practical understanding of the Spirit's movement in the church, especially the spiritual experiences of our youth group, "Guerreros Conquistadores."

My years at the Hispanic Institute of Ministry in Dallas, Texas, were a time of drinking from the wells of Pentecostal heritage. There, I had various pastor/teachers who fostered in me a sense of the importance of practical theologizing and a love for church ministry. In particular, two Hispanic Pentecostal instructors and scholars helped to shape my early theological reflection. Sergio Farias inspired me to want to teach in an academic setting; his quick wit and funny anecdotes made our classes enjoyable, and his desire for academic excellence provided us a model to follow. Dr. Hiram Almirudis's love of the Scriptures (especially the Greek text, which seemed never to leave his side) introduced me to a world of scholarship I had previously not known. It was in a conversation with him that I first made plans to continue my education and dreamt of obtaining a doctorate. He not only served as a spiritual and academic mentor, but also supported me financially through scholarships his sons funded. Muchisisimas gracias!

Another special group of people that I want to recognize is the Pentecostal women scholars who guided my thinking. First and foremost, my mother, Alicia Gil Alfaro, has always been a source of inspiration. Before she married, she attended the Bible Institute Berea (Hermosillo, Sonora, Mexico), where she so excelled in the eyes of the administration and faculty that she became an instructor at the very early age of 17. She educated many young pastors who later became prominent and influential leaders within the Spanish-speaking Church of God (Cleveland, TN). In part, my work is a tribute to her desire for one of her children to attend the Bible Institute ("lo hice y un poco más!"). Among other women scholars who have nurtured my thought, I am grateful for having studied with Dr. Rebecca Skaggs and Dr. Hannah Harrington, both professors at Patten University (Oakland, CA). They were my private tutors in Greek and Hebrew, respectively, and allowed me to take coursework with them in their offices (and even their homes) when low enrollment prevented courses from running. In appreciation of this gesture and in imitation of their servant leadership, I will always have an open heart, office, and home for students.

I owe much appreciation also to my professors at Fuller Theological Seminary. I have learned from all of you the importance of balancing faith and reason, and to recognize that what we do in academia should always be in service to the church. As representatives of the Fuller faculty, I point to Dr. Colin Brown and Dr. Veli-Matti Kärkkäinen. Dr. Brown, thank you for taking me as a student when my application fell on your desk, after being rejected twice due to my lack of discernment. It has surely been an honor to be mentored by you, and to learn from you humility and excellence in scholarship. Dr. Kärkkäinen, you have modeled for me what it means to be a Pentecostal and a scholar; to never separate the two and to let each enrich the other.

A special acknowledgment is also in order for the Hispanic Theological Initiative, a program that provided me with a community of Hispanic scholars whom I have come to consider my academic familia. Joanne, your support was priceless; you fought for me and opened rivers of financial blessing from unexpected sources. Maria, te considero como la tía chévere de la familia de HTI; siempre me animaste con una sonrisa y un caluroso saludo. Angela, your diligence and attention to detail always made for prompt disbursements and a great sigh of relief on our part. Efrain, you mentored me "in season and out of season," and your friendship was a valuable resource for navigating through the doctoral program. Uli, you have taught me the value of critical and expert eyes looking over what I write; my best writing in this project is because of you (but any errors continue to be mine).

Last, and most important of all, I want to thank my family for their continued support and prayers, which were my source of strength in finishing this project. David and Marissa, you were both born during my years in the doctoral program, and, though you were not aware of it at the time, you were a constant source of motivation. David, I cared for you while I studied for French and prepared for comprehensive exams, and you helped to de-stress my mind after long hours of writing. Marissa, I began writing my dissertation shortly before we knew we were expecting you, but you began walking before I finished writing— that was our first race, and you beat me! May you both excel in everything you do and help each other in every accomplishment. Miriam, you have sacrificed a great deal to get me to this point. We started dating just before I began studying at the Bible Institute, and have been with me every step of the way. Thank you for all the support and love you have given me on this journey. May the rest of our journey be just as pleasant and joyful.

Abbreviations

AF   *The Apostolic Faith*, edited by William Seymour.
            Periodical of the Azusa Street Mission.

BM   *The Bridegroom's Messenger*, edited by G. B. Cashwell
            and Elizabeth A. Sexton.

CGE   *Church of God Evangel*, edited by A. J. Tomlinson and
            Sam Perry. Periodical of the Pentecostal denomina-
            tion the Church of God (Cleveland, TN).

JPTSup   Journal of Pentecostal Theology Supplement Series,
            edited by John Christopher Thomas, Rickie D.
            Moore, and Steven J. Land.

JPT   *Journal of Pentecostal Theology*

NIDPCM   *The New International Dictionary of Pentecostal
            and Charismatic Movements*, edited by Stanley M.
            Burgess and Eduard M. Van der Maas (Grand Rapids:
            Zondervan, 2002).

PE   *Pentecostal Evangel*, periodical of the Assemblies of
            God (Springfield, MI).

Pneuma   *Pneuma: The Journal of the Society for Pentecostal
            Studies*

Introduction

CONSIDERING THE PHENOMENAL GROWTH OF PENTECOSTALISM[1] IN
the last century[2] and the fact an overwhelming majority of its adherents belong to the "Two-Thirds World,"[3] it is no surprise that many

1. At the outset of this study I want to clarify that "Pentecostalism" will be used inclusively of Charismatics and Neocharismatics; whereas "Pentecostal" will refer to the classical origins of the movement at the beginning of the twentieth century, and the denominations and theologians who continue to work within that doctrinal tradition. This study will follow the threefold typology (Pentecostal/Charismatic/Neocharismatic) developed in *The New International Dictionary of Pentecostal and Charismatic Movements* (hereafter abbreviated *NIDPCM*). In this consensual analysis, "Classical Pentecostals" refers to the movements that trace their origins to the early twentieth-century "outpourings of the Spirit," of which the Azusa Street Revival is representative. Second, "Charismatics" or the "Charismatic Movement" refers to the spiritual renewal ("an increased interest in Spiritual gifts, including *glossolalia* [speaking in tongues], prophecy, and physical healing") that occurred within the Catholic and mainline Protestant churches beginning in 1960. Third, "Neocharismatics" refers to the numerous movements ("18,810 independent, indigenous, and postdenominational denominations") that cannot be classified as either Pentecostal or Charismatic, but "share a common emphasis on the Holy Spirit, spiritual gifts, Pentecostal-like experiences (not Pentecostal terminology), signs and wonders, and power encounters." *NIDPCM*, xvii–xxii.

2. For the last one hundred years Pentecostalism has grown from being a seemingly insignificant offshoot of the Revivalist and Holiness movements to becoming a global force within Christendom today. Some estimate that Pentecostalism accounts for about one-fourth of the total Christian population in the world. A very elaborate survey of Pentecostal/Charismatic global statistics, accompanied with summary notes and tables, is provided in *NIDPCM*, 284–302.

3. The term "Third World" is a pejorative descriptor, because it denotes a hierarchical relation between the more "developed" and powerful nations (the "First World") in contrast to those that are less "developed" and significantly weaker. I prefer the more positive "Two-Thirds World" because it highlights the fact that two-thirds of the world's population inhabits the so-called Third World, and, therefore, it is the majority. This is significant when considering the reception of Pentecostalism in the Two-Thirds World. It is a matter of great debate whether Pentecostalism had its origins in North America or sprouted simultaneously yet independently in various places around the world at the beginning of the twentieth century. However, there is no doubt that "Pentecostalism is strongest now in the so-called 'Third World.'" Land, *Pentecostal Spirituality*, 21.

within the movement, and even some from without,[4] have called for a Pentecostal theology that takes into account the social context of the Pentecostal community of faith. Reflecting on the theological task from a Pentecostal perspective, Steven Land considers that the "explosive growth [of Pentecostalism] in the Third World" necessitates a careful response to "new and urgent questions of theology, discipleship and suffering."[5] Indeed, given the constantly increasing number of Pentecostal believers outside the borders of the U.S., it is crucial that Pentecostal theology, if it desires to speak in light of its global presence, take seriously the social location of the majority of its membership.[6]

Considering the geographical location and social context of Pentecostals, Charismatics, and Neocharismatics combined, it is highly significant that 66 percent of these live in the Two-Thirds World, and that 87 percent live in poverty. Barrett and Johnson, "Global Statistics," 284.

4. Catholic scholars in Latin America, as well as in the U.S., have long spoken about the challenge of Pentecostalism. The rapid growth of Pentecostalism in Latin America, sometimes referred to as the "Pentecostalization of Latin America," has caused liberationist theologians to reconsider its religious, political, and theological impact. Significantly, the combined presence of Latin American Charismatic Catholics and Latin American Pentecostals accounts for 27 percent of the Latin American population, while in the U.S. the combined presence of Latina/o Charismatic Catholics and Latina/o Pentecostals accounts for 28 percent of the Latina/o population. See Wilson, "Latin American Pentecostals," 85–90; Alvarez, "Latin American Pentecostals," 91–95; Deck, "Challenge of Evangelical Pentecostal Christianity"; and Espinosa, "Pentecostalization of Latin America."

5. Land, *Pentecostal Spirituality*, 191. Significantly, Amos Yong begins his proposal for "a world Pentecostal theology by focusing on the phenomenology of Pentecostalisms in Latin America, Asia and Africa" Yong, *Spirit Poured Out*, 32. His reasoning includes the notion that "North American Pentecostalism is no longer at the vanguard of what God is doing through this movement in the world" (ibid.). Yong concludes that since "there is already the clear connection between Pentecostalism and the poor, disenfranchised, and marginalized of the world," Pentecostal theology must reflect a liberative approach. Ibid., 80. Two other notable scholars who consider the growth of Pentecostalism in the Two-Thirds World as both challenge and promise not only to Pentecostal theology itself, but also to the study of religion, are Harvey Cox and Walter J. Hollenweger. See Cox, *Fire from Heaven*, 317–20; and Hollenweger, *Pentecostalism*, 1–2; idem, "Pentecostal Elites, 200–214.

6. Although there are virtually hundreds of Pentecostal denominations and independent churches worldwide, not to mention the thousands of Neocharismatic movements, three of the oldest classic Pentecostal denominations (Assemblies of God, Church of God [Cleveland, TN], Church of God in Prophecy), which have their headquarters in the U.S., have governing bodies that consist predominantly of white men. Significantly, within the mentioned denominations, Hispanic congregations have outgrown their Anglo counterparts, and yet they continue to be underrepresented in

The Need for a Pentecostal Christology

As a result of Pentecostalism's global growth in the past few decades, the production of theological works from a Pentecostal perspective with a focus on social concern and liberative praxis has increased in Latin America, Asia, and Africa.[7] There has also been a rise in theological writings by Black and Asian Pentecostal scholars in the U.S., whose contribution reminds us that everyone does theology from a specific social location.[8] From a Hispanic perspective, two such works are particularly important: Samuel Solivan's *The Spirit, Pathos and Liberation* (1998) and Eldin Villafañe's *The Liberating Spirit* (1992). Apart from these, regrettably, Hispanic Pentecostal theologians have yet to produce works that set out to do theology from their own unique perspective and focus on systematic theology themes beyond pneumatology, such as Christology, soteriology, ecclesiology, and eschatology. Thus, whereas one can say Latino theology has come of age, Hispanic Pentecostal theology seems to have remained in a state of infancy, yet to develop to a full-fledged theology.[9]

---

higher church leadership. A recent newspaper article attributes the rapid growth of Pentecostal churches to the increasing conversion of Hispanics from Catholicism to Pentecostalism, especially new immigrants to the U.S. Innes, "Hispanics Fuel Growth in Pentecostal Churches." This is statistically substantiated by Jesse Miranda and E. L. Wilson, who estimate that "between 1980 and 1997, the number of Hispanic congregations in the AG [Assemblies of God] grew from 1,100 to 1,723 (56.7%), while membership grew from 93,000 to 178,017 (91.2%). In the meantime, the congregation and membership in the Anglo geographical districts increased by, respectively, 17.2% and 7.7%." Miranda and Wilson, "Hispanic Pentecostalism," 716. In this same article, they go on to document similar figures for the Church of God (Cleveland, TN) and report that this tendency applies to other denominations, including the Church of the Foursquare Gospel, the Church of God of Prophesy, and the United Pentecostals.

7. Pentecostal theologies from Latin America include: Alvarez, ed., *Pentecostalism y Liberación*; Mariz, *Coping with Poverty*; Peterson, *Not by Might Nor by Power*; and Gutierrez and Smith, eds., *In the Power of the Spirit*. Moreover, the existence of the *Asian Journal of Pentecostal Studies* testifies to the concern for doing theology from a specific perspective. For a sampling of Asian Pentecostal theology, see Anderson and Tang, eds., *Asian and Pentecostal*. Concerning African Pentecostal theologies, consult Gifford, "Complex Provenance."

8. For extensive bibliographies, see Phan, *Christianity with an Asian Face*; and Sanders, *Saints in Exile*.

9. In part this lack of theological production corresponds to the traditional anti-intellectualism that has characterized the Pentecostal community from its origins until today. In turn this amounts to a double whammy when considering Hispanic

It is no surprise the existing theological works from a Hispanic Pentecostal perspective center on pneumatology; a movement so focused on the work of the Spirit and the Pentecostal gifts would be expected to give prominence to the life of the Spirit. Furthermore, it is rational to begin our theological reflections on the subject of the Spirit, for there has been much work dedicated to constructing Pentecostal theology beginning with the third article of the Apostles' Creed ("I believe in the Holy Spirit").[10] Yet, though the idea of pneumatology being the driving force behind all Pentecostal theology makes sense, Pentecostal beliefs have traditionally been richly christological in nature, and for that reason Pentecostals do well to realize pneumatology need not eclipse Christology because in fact the two go hand in hand.

Since its origins, Pentecostal spirituality has been characterized by a christocentric worship and experience. In accordance with this experience, the central theme of Pentecostal reflection is Jesus Christ, which is concretely evidenced in the portrayal of the Fivefold Gospel (i.e., the understanding of Jesus as Savior, Healer, Sanctifier, Baptizer, and Soon-Coming King).[11] Given the christocentric nature of Pentecostal thought and worship, one may wonder why a distinctive Christology from a Pentecostal perspective has yet to appear; and even more so for a community that lives, breathes, and walks in the presence of Jesus

Pentecostals' disadvantaged position and their difficulty in attaining higher education. Still, there is hope in light of the increasing participation of Hispanic Pentecostals in the academy, especially in regard to the Society of Pentecostal Studies and journals that promote the scholarly study of Pentecostalism.

10. In 1957 Karl Barth made some comments regarding the possibility of reconceptualizing Christian systematic theology with a pneumatological orientation. He said, "There is certainly a place for legitimate Christian thinking starting from below and moving up, from man who is taken hold of God to God who takes hold of man . . . one might well understand it as a theology of the third article . . . Starting from below, as it were, with Christian man, it could and should have struggled its way upward to an authentic explication of the Christian faith." Barth, "Evangelical Theology," 24–25. Responding to Barth's seminal thoughts, within the Pentecostal/Charismatic academy various articles and chapters in books have recently appeared to flesh out this motif. For example, D. Lyle Dabney outlines the contours of a "third article theology" in "Why Should the Last Be First?"

11. Donald Dayton rightly traces the origins of Pentecostalism's Fivefold Gospel to A. B. Simpson's (founder of the Christian Missionary Alliance) fourfold understanding of the full gospel: Jesus as Savior, Sanctifier, Healer, and Soon-Coming King. The significance and effects of Pentecostalism's novel inclusion of Jesus as Baptizer will be discussed in chapter 1.

through the Spirit. The challenge of this study is precisely this: to inquire about the foundations needed to construct a Hispanic Pentecostal Christology that is rooted in the experience of the Hispanic community and developed with an interest toward a liberative praxis.

Significantly, Pentecostals have always emphasized a Christology with soteriological concerns that are not confined to the spiritual realm, but having effects on the body in the form of healings and deliverance.[12] However, due to an almost wholesale appropriation of a forensic atonement theory, and though healing and deliverance came to be understood as provided for in the atonement, the social dimension of salvation is almost completely ignored.[13] And yet, given the context of extreme poverty in which the majority of Pentecostal believers subsist, it becomes crucial to understand Christian salvation in more holistic terms, which include, though are not limited to, liberative praxis.[14]

In part, the reason for Pentecostalism's confinement of salvation mostly to the spiritual realm is the limited nature of its main christological model. Traditionally Pentecostal Christology has been anchored in a two-natures Chalcedonian Christology, which exhibits a soteriological emphasis governed by the need to demonstrate the legitimacy of Jesus' salvific work in light of his divinity on the one hand and his humanity on the other; he had to be divine in order to save and human in order to save *us*. This study proposes that Spirit-Christology, a model oriented to "theological reflection on the role of the Holy Spirit in Christology

12. In her thorough investigation of Pentecostal healing, Kimberly Ervin Alexander summarizes, "the doctrine of Divine Healing in the Atonement was understood [by early Pentecostals] as part and parcel of salvation. As a provision of the Atonement, and as part of Christ's 'two-fold' ministry, healing is a necessary ingredient of what it means to be holy and whole." Alexander, *Pentecostal Healing*, 53. See also Menzies and Menzies, "Healing in the Atonement," 159–70.

13. For example, Daniel B. Pecota considers the saving work of Christ without any mention of how it might affect the social sphere. In this sense, Christian "salvation" is understood as operative only in the spiritual sphere, with some overflow into the corporal dimension in healing and deliverance from the demonic. Thus, his treatment of theories of atonement reflects an individualistic understanding of salvation where the corporate dimension is completely avoided. Pecota, "Saving Work of Christ," 325–73.

14. Helpful in this regard is the analysis of Gustavo Gutierrez on Christ and integral liberation: "salvation embraces all persons and the whole person; the liberating action of Christ—made human in *this* history and not in a history marginal to real human life—is at the heart of the historical current of humanity; the struggle for a just society is in its own right very much a part of salvation history." Gutierrez, *Theology of Liberation*, 97; emphasis added.

proper,"[15] is more suitable for constructing a Hispanic Pentecostal Christology, provided it is grounded in the experience, faith, and worship of the Hispanic Pentecostal community and oriented toward liberative praxis. I contend that by adopting a two-natures Chalcedonian model the development of a distinctive Pentecostal Christology was hindered in early Pentecostal writings, as in later Pentecostal systematic theologies and even in more recent attempts. Instead of continuing in an unproductive way, Hispanic Pentecostal Christology would do well to consider Spirit-Christology as a complementary paradigm for developing a Christology that is not only categorically pneumatological but also truly Pentecostal. In order to address the perceived limitations of Spirit-Christology, I will turn to Latina/o Christologies as a resource for doing theology from the context of the Latina/o experience in the U.S. Thus, by building on the Pentecostal heritage and supplementing Spirit-Christology by the insights from Latina/o Christologies, I propose to move toward a relevant Hispanic Pentecostal Christology.

Review of Related Literature

Research on this topic quickly confirms the suspicion that Pentecostals, for the most part, have only focused on Christology in a tangential manner. Whereas books and articles pertaining to pneumatology abound, scholarly treatments of Christology from a Pentecostal perspective are lacking.[16] Even the Christologies of Pentecostal systematic theologies and recent theological works are more soteriological or pneumatological in focus. One might even say that the former are not characteristically Pentecostal, for they merely seem to mimic evangelical systematic Christologies.

Why is there this theological subordination of Christology to pneumatology within a movement that from its inception has sought to be centered on Christ? Could it be that Christology for Pentecostals

---

15. Ralph Del Colle's definition in *Christ and the Spirit*, 3. He goes on to say that Spirit-Christology "seeks to understand both 'who Christ is' and 'what Christ has done' from the perspective of the third article of the creed: 'I believe in the Holy Spirit, the Lord and Giver of Life.'"

16. Pointing to the absence of a contemporary Pentecostal Christology, Veli-Matti Kärkkäinen comments in his survey of global Christologies, the Pentecostal tradition is not represented "for the simple reason that a specifically Pentecostal christologist has yet to appear." Kärkkäinen, *Christology*, 110.

is approached differently? One must acknowledge that, as opposed to a more systematic approach, Pentecostals have a different method for working out Christology. Nevertheless, the lack of christological production within Pentecostal theology is a significant thematic gap that needs to be addressed. Especially because a main task of the Spirit is to glorify Christ, a main task for Pentecostal theology today should also be to work out a Christology that focuses concretely on Jesus' person, life, and work from its unique Pentecostal standpoint.

What is even more striking is that the turn toward Spirit-Christology has been a topic of discussion for quite some time now, and yet no thorough Pentecostal Christology has surfaced. For example, the Roman Catholic charismatic theologian Ralph Del Colle insists that "Spirit-Christology is the most productive systematic christological model by which to understand and inform the unique contributions of Pentecostal-charismatic spirituality to the church catholic."[17] In this article, he defines Spirit-Christology as "envisioning the constitution and mission of the person of Christ in terms that establish an interrelationship between the filiological and the pneumatological dimensions of Christology."[18] By this he means to highlight the Trinitarian dimensions of Christology as found in the gospel accounts of the life of Jesus; Jesus is both "Son" and "Spirit-bearer." Del Colle further explains the significance of Spirit-Christology for Pentecostals, saying,

> To contemplate the person of Jesus Christ in light of the Pentecostal-charismatic experience is to explicate the confession of 'truly human' and 'truly divine' within the ambit of a Spirit-anointed and transfigured human being that is God's communicative and salvific relation to humanity. He is the mediator of life, mission and our deepest human identity, what we can describe in the language of election as our calling to exist in graced filial relation to God.[19]

What this quotation reveals is how the Pentecostal experience of the Spirit serves as a vantage point for discerning Jesus' identity and relation to God as a true human. Thus, it is Jesus' humanity in the Spirit that becomes the focus of Pentecostal Christology.

17. Del Colle, "Spirit-Christology," 92–93.

18. Ibid., 93.

19. Ibid., 93–94.

In light of Del Colle's proposal, Pentecostal theologian Harold Hunter, who had previously bemoaned Spirit-Christology as an unorthodox paradigm for Christology, later came to regard it in more positive terms. In an excursus in his doctoral dissertation, he analyzed current models of Spirit-Christology and found them unsatisfactory, for in his appraisal they questioned the divinity of Jesus and reduced the Spirit to a divine influence.[20] However, a decade after his indictment of Spirit-Christology, Hunter revisited it and concluded that so long as "Christology and Pneumatology are seen in the framework of a Trinitarian structure that embraces both," Spirit-Christology can be a useful paradigm.[21]

In similar fashion, it has been argued more recently that Spirit-Christology need not become a replacement model for Logos Christology, but that the former complements the later. This is the road taken by both Myk Habets and Steven M. Studebaker.[22] The crucial connection that both of them make is that Spirit-Christology needs to be driven by a Trinitarian framework in order to avoid both denying the full divinity of Jesus Christ, on the one hand, and equating the Spirit with merely a power or influence, on the other.

Another recent Pentecostal work on Christology is worth noting: S. D. L. Jenkins's doctoral dissertation, "The Human Son of God and the Holy Spirit." This work is perhaps the only sustained scholarly writing from a Pentecostal perspective that argues for the adoption of Spirit-Christology as a complementary model to the traditional Logos-Christologies developed by the early church fathers.[23] According to Jenkins the role of Spirit-Christology is not only to supplement, but more "to revise traditional christological formulations."[24] Such efforts, however, need not result in either an Adoptionist Christology, where

20. Hunter, *Spirit-Baptism*, 225.

21. Hunter, "Resurgence of Spirit Christology."

22. See Habets, "Spirit Christology"; and Studebaker, "Integrating Pneumatology and Christology." Both of these studies will be critically evaluated in chapter 3.

23. Other such proposals have appeared from scholars who are sympathetic to the Pentecostal movement. These works will provide the nucleus for developing a Spirit-Christology from a Pentecostal perspective. Illustrative of these, one can point to the already mentioned Roman Catholic and Charismatic scholar Ralph Del Colle (under whom Jenkins wrote his dissertation), who has continually invited Pentecostals to turn toward Spirit-Christology as a model for their own distinctive Christology. See Del Colle, *Christ and the Spirit*.

24. Jenkins, "Human Son of God," 2.

Jesus' divinity is completely lacking, nor a binitarian Christology, where the Spirit is simply the functional principle of Jesus' divinity. In contrast, Jenkins opts for a Trinitarian Christology, which attempts to understand the nature of Jesus and his works from the standpoint of his relationship to both the Father and the Spirit.

Realizing the lack of theological rigor in the writings of early Pentecostalism, Jenkins turns to recent approaches to Spirit-Christology in order to strengthen his perception that the model is more in line with Pentecostal reflection on the person and work of Jesus. Central to his thesis is the analysis of the proto-Pentecostal Edward Irving (1792–1834) who anticipated the Pentecostal movement in his practice (e.g., speaking in tongues and healing) and theological musings (e.g., the development of baptism with the Spirit doctrine).[25] Irving becomes Jenkins's primary dialogue partner as he turns to more recent works on Spirit-Christology.

Although I will briefly analyze his work later in chapter three, at this point my concern with Jenkins's project is that he dismisses early Pentecostal reflection of Jesus too quickly. He does include a chapter on early Pentecostalism's incipient Spirit-Christology, but his exploration is limited in that he discusses only three periodicals: *The Apostolic Faith*, *The Bridegroom's Messenger*, and the *Church of God Evangel*. It is my conviction that a more thorough analysis of early Pentecostal writings would confirm the suspicion that Spirit-Christology is indeed a better paradigm for Pentecostal Christology and would obviate turning to sources predating the Pentecostal movement. Nevertheless, I believe the strength of Jenkins's work is its ecumenical nature, for he intends to bring Pentecostal Christology in the making into dialogue with the recent evangelical and Roman Catholic proposals for Spirit-Christology.

The Nature of Pentecostal Theology

In light of Jenkins's proposal, it becomes significant to ask what makes Pentecostal theology Pentecostal. Does it mean to simply reproduce or systematize the theological thinking of early Pentecostalism? Is it enough to be a Pentecostal who theologizes in dialogue with past and recent theological traditions and scholars? Just how does one go about

---

25. For a brief yet detailed description of his life, ministry, and theological writings see, Bundy, "Irving, Edward," 803–4.

doing Pentecostal theology? Because my overall aim is to develop a Pentecostal theology, I believe it would be helpful to briefly describe its nature, in order to see how it relates to the method of this study.

The distinguishing element that set apart Pentecostalism from the various branches of Holiness Movements at the beginning of the twentieth-century was "the experience of speaking in tongues as the evidence of having received the baptism with the Holy Spirit."[26] One can say that speaking in tongues was the final push in the "back to Pentecost" movement initiated by John Wesley and carried forth by his followers and later revivalists. As Steven J. Land states, early Pentecostals believed that God had been restoring the apostolic faith with concern to signs and wonders, just as

> God had restored justification by faith through Luther, sanctification by faith through Wesley, divine healing through Dr Cullis and many other nineteenth-century ministers, the blessed hope of Christ's pre-millennial second coming through the prophecy conferences of the latter half of the nineteenth century, and lastly the baptism in the Holy Spirit as power for the last-days world evangelization.[27]

It was not enough simply to believe in the baptism of the Holy Spirit as enabling Christians for evangelistic work; the experience of speaking in tongues was the visible sign of the church's journey "back to Pentecost." Concerning speaking in tongues, one might ask: what came first, the experience or the belief? Was there already a clearly outlined system of thought that heralded the experience of speaking in tongues? Or did the experience of speaking in tongues demand a theological explanation?

In a sense, one can say that the theological baggage early Pentecostals inherited led them to the threshold of Pentecostalism, but that the experience of speaking in tongues pushed them through the door—and one might add, closed the door behind them. Pentecostal theology, then and now, contains fundamental elements that bind it closely to evangelical theology; yet, is distinguished from the latter by the doctrine of speaking in tongues as evidence (initial and continuing) of the baptism of/ with the Holy Spirit. Since the Pentecostal imagination emerged within

26. Dayton, *Theological Roots of Pentecostalism*, 176.

27. Land, *Pentecostal Spirituality*, 18. Here Land is paraphrasing a passage from Seymour, "Pentecostal Baptism Restored."

the cradle of American Revivalism and the Holiness movement, it is no surprise that from them it inherited a particular way of doing theology. However, due to the added framework needed for understanding the experience of the baptism with the Holy Spirit, one must ask what unique elements give shape to theological method from a Pentecostal perspective.

It has been argued that traditionally Pentecostals have not focused on theological method, and have simply borrowed alien "methodological thought structures" to give shape to their Pentecostal reflections.[28] Moreover, as various early Pentecostal sermons could testify, others argue, early Pentecostals were not interested so much in theology as they were in biblical theology or doctrine.[29] But should such a distinction be made between biblical doctrine and the more "academic" notion of systematic theology? Compared to the contemporaneous fundamentalist approach to theology, Harvey Cox describes the Pentecostal way of doing theology like this:

> The difference is that while the beliefs of the fundamentalists, and of many other religious groups, are enshrined in formal theological systems, those of pentecostalism are imbedded in testimonies, ecstatic speech, and bodily movement. But it *is* a theology, a full-blown religious cosmos, an intricate system of symbols that respond to the perennial questions of human meaning and value. The difference is that, historically, pentecostals have felt more at home singing their theology, or putting it in pamphlets for distribution on streets corners. Only recently have they begun writing books about it.[30]

Whatever early Pentecostals' self-understanding was as regards making sense of Scripture (i.e., "dividing rightly the Word of God," or simply, biblical doctrine), one thing is certain: though they might have sought to avoid being labeled theologians, inescapably they elaborated theo-

---

28. Stephenson, "Rule of Spirituality," 84.

29. The following quotation is an example of the sort of anti-intellectual attitude (or, put positively, the desire to disassociate the Pentecostal approach to understanding Scripture from what they conceived as being purely academic theologizing) of early Pentecostals: "God does not need a great theological preacher that can give anything but theological chips and shaving to people. He can pick up a worm and trash a mountain . . ." Seymour, "Back to Pentecost."

30. Cox, *Fire from Heaven*, 15.

logical thoughts, and as such could and should be labeled rightly as theologians of the Spirit.

The fact is that Pentecostal beliefs were not without a theological foundation that rested concretely on the testimony of Scripture. It is no less a theological affirmation to state one can speak of God as Trinitarian because he exists in three persons than to say the baptism of the Holy Spirit is available for believers today. Furthermore, one cannot chidingly label the latter as simply a confessional statement without applying the same rhetoric to the former. Theological affirmations do not need to be backed up by a faculty position or a degree from a theological institution. In order to appreciate the theological understanding of early Pentecostals, one has to begin by shedding the prejudice that they acted without any need for theological constructs. That they approached the Bible (and one might say theology) in a different manner is not tantamount to their having a lack of concern for a theological framework.

To illustrate the need to understand Pentecostal theology on its own terms, one can point to the debate between Lyle Dabney and Veli-Matti Kärkkäinen.[31] Dabney argues Pentecostal theology cannot afford to simply take up the tools of other traditions in order to craft its own theological framework, for in the end this would serve to drown out the distinctiveness of the Pentecostal tradition in a way that parallels Saul's action of placing his armor on David.[32] Kärkkäinen's response is that in the quest for theological identity "Pentecostal theology should [not] be so 'Pentecostal' that it becomes a theology on its own terms," and considers, "Pentecostalism should not major so much on crafting its own theological methodology . . . but rather should join hands with other theological traditions to work toward a more comprehensive, contextually sensitive theological model."[33] I wonder, however, if the two positions are able to balance each other. On the one hand, we need

31. The conversation centers around the publication of Kärkkäinen's two significant works on the Roman Catholic–Pentecostal dialogue, *Spiritus ubi vult spirat* and *Ad ultimum terrae*. Dabney's review includes an exploration into the implications of these books for Pentecostal theology, and is followed by Kärkkäinen's response. See Dabney, "Saul's Armor"; and Kärkkäinen, "David's Sling."

32. Dabney, "Saul's Armor," 116–17.

33. In all fairness, we need to understand Kärkkäinen's comments as flowing from his ecumenical concern, as he makes sure to point out. See Kärkkäinen, "David's Sling," 150.

not abandon the quest for a uniquely Pentecostal theological method, for our contribution to other traditions can only be made if we first take our own distinctive theological perspective seriously. On the other hand, we cannot develop our methods in isolation from the history of theology, for it helpfully serves to enrich and critique our pneumatological inclinations.

Methodology

I aim in this book to establish foundations for constructing a Hispanic Pentecostal Christology that is oriented toward liberative practice. Key for my purpose is a constructive approach that aims at bringing together recent approaches to Spirit-Christology and the contextual/liberative hermeneutics of Latina/o theologies. Thus, although traditionally Pentecostal Christologies have been anchored in a two-natures Chalcedonian model, this study will show that Spirit Christology is a more suitable paradigm for constructing a Hispanic Pentecostal Christology, provided it is grounded in the experience, faith, and worship of its community and oriented toward liberative praxis. My method is as follows:

The first chapter will outline early Pentecostal Christology, demonstrating that Spirit-Christology is a more suitable model for constructing a Pentecostal Christology today. This chapter will focus almost entirely on early Pentecostal writings (e.g., articles and sermons appearing in early Pentecostal periodicals) that reflect on the person and work of Jesus Christ. In order to organize early Pentecostal Christology, I will use the Fivefold model of Savior, Sanctifier, Baptizer, Healer, and Soon-Coming King, showing how the relation of Jesus and the Spirit becomes a central motif in the christological reflection of early Pentecostals. This chapter will also argue that the more unique elements of Pentecostal Christology (especially in their relation to Spirit-Christology) were largely left unexplored in light of challenges posed by the Oneness movement and the adoption of a two-natures Chalcedonian Christology. The primary aim of this chapter will be to establish the move toward Spirit-Christology as a legitimate one due to our Pentecostal heritage.

In chapter two, I look at the recent Pentecostal turn toward Spirit-Christology. Before doing this, however, I will argue Pentecostals need to move beyond a Chalcedonian model, although it should continue to complement Spirit-Christology. Then, the biblical and early-church foundations for Spirit-Christology will be explored as a way to highlight what the model has to offer. Next, non-Pentecostal models of Spirit-Christology will be examined in order to elucidate the various controversial christological debates and some proposed solutions that have surged in the last decades. Following this section, I will survey some Pentecostal proposals for Spirit-Christology that aim to develop the contours for a Pentecostal Christology. Before ending this chapter, though, I will return to the issue of the Oneness view of Jesus and explore the potential solutions that Spirit-Christology might offer to this extremely sensitive and difficult intra-Pentecostal debate.

Instead of moving directly toward the construction of a Hispanic Pentecostal Christology, however, another resource will be tapped into in the third chapter. The reason for this is that, though Spirit-Christology proves to be a useful model for constructing a Pentecostal Christology in general, for it to be a viable model for Hispanic Pentecostal Christology it needs to be contextually grounded and oriented toward liberative praxis. Accordingly, this chapter will examine the contributions of Latin American and Latina/o Christologies as resources for contextually grounding Spirit-Christology and orienting it toward liberative praxis. Key in this respect is the liberative christological imagination of Latin American and Hispanic thinkers, an imagination that proclaims a Jesus who enters the barrio and transforms it. Due to the social location of Hispanics (Catholic and Protestant alike) and particularly the demographics of Hispanic Pentecostals, the christological contributions of Latina/o theologians will prove essential for developing a Hispanic Pentecostal christological method that aims to integrate faith and lived experience of Jesus in a context of economic hardship, transnational ambivalence, and continual marginalization.

All the pieces of the puzzle will be put together in chapter four, "*Divino Compañero*: Toward a Hispanic Pentecostal Christology." By bringing together the foundational elements of early Pentecostal Christology (its fivefold model) along with insights of recent Pentecostal Spirit-Christologies and the contributions of Latina/o Christologies, this chapter develops a historically grounded Spirit-Christology of liberative praxis that is relevant for Hispanic Pentecostals today. The central image of this Christology is El Divino Compañero, for in Pentecostals' pilgrimage through this world it is Jesus, the Divine Companion, who through the Spirit guides and nurtures them on the way back home. This last chapter asks: In light of the context of Hispanic Pentecostals, what are the key christological themes that continue to frame the understanding of the person and work of Jesus? In short, who is Jesus Christ for Hispanic Pentecostals today?

Essentially, I look back at the christological reflection of early Pentecostals and the contemporary turn to Spirit-Christology, and then construct a christological model that is born out of the Hispanic Pentecostal reality, but is also rooted in the broader Pentecostal christological imagination and informed by the Pentecostal way of doing theology. I believe a Hispanic Pentecostal Spirit-Christology has the potential to model a new way of doing Christology: an approach that is globally conscious and praxis oriented and that attempts to conceptualize the meaning of the person and work of Christ with biblical centeredness.

1

Early Pentecostal Christology

Despite the centrality of Jesus in Pentecostal worship, belief, and practice, from an academic perspective Christology has been an underdeveloped theological theme in Pentecostalism.[1] And yet just because Pentecostals have concentrated almost exclusively on pneumatology does not mean that Pentecostalism lacks a distinctive Christology. From its origins, Pentecostal writings, sermons, and testimonies reveal a unique way of thinking about the person and work of Jesus Christ, one which stresses the continued active presence of the second person of the Trinity in the life of the church and the believer. Pentecostal Christology affirms that Jesus Christ is the same yesterday, today, and forever (Heb 13:8); this same miracle-working preacher-prophet continues to manifest his presence through the Spirit today.

This chapter analyzes a sampling of early Pentecostal writings in order to show that Spirit-Christology is a viable model for constructing a Christology rooted in the Pentecostal tradition. The data for this research comes primarily from articles that appeared in the earliest Pentecostal periodicals, and, to a lesser degree, Pentecostal tracts and books written in its "period of formulation" (1901–1929).[2] The reason

1. Pointing to the absence of a contemporary Pentecostal Christology, Veli-Matti Kärkkäinen comments that in his survey of global Christologies the Pentecostal tradition is not represented "for the simple reason that a specifically Pentecostal christologist has yet to appear." Kärkkäinen, *Christology*, 110.

2. Paul W. Lewis uses the phrase "period of formulation" to refer to the period when "the foundational elements of Pentecostal thought were developed and established." The dates used to bookend this formative phase refer to notable events in the Pentecostal movement. The year 1901 refers to Agnes Ozman's experience of receiving the Holy Spirit with the initial evidence of speaking in tongues. This is the first such experience as understood in classical Pentecostal terms. The year 1929 refers to the death of

for limiting the study in this way is because it was during the first ten years of the Pentecostal movement (1906–1916) that the distinctiveness of Pentecostal faith and practice was established.[3] Also, because the Pentecostal tradition was steeped in oral tradition, with a special focus on the experience of the Pentecostal gifts, the key sources in recovering these foundations are found not so much in theological treatises (as in other traditions) but rather in articles and sermons. Thus, one can obtain a good grasp of early Pentecostal thinking on any theological subject matter by analyzing popular writings that are representative of the various Pentecostal movements.

This chapter proceeds as follows: First, I analyze the christological inheritance of Pentecostalism and its distinctive approach to Christology. Next, I organize early Pentecostal christological themes into a cohesive model by following the common Fivefold Gospel rubric developed in early Pentecostalism (i.e., Jesus as Savior, Sanctifier, Baptizer, Healer, and Soon-Coming King). I end the chapter by demonstrating how the challenge presented by Oneness Christology resulted in the adoption of a Chalcedonian two-natures Christology, which limited the development of a distinctive Pentecostal Christology. Overall, my aim is to show that Spirit-Christology serves as a model for constructing a Pentecostal Christology that is true to its heritage.

The Christological Core of Early Pentecostal Thought

In his book *Pentecostal Spirituality*, Steven J. Land describes the religious affections of early Pentecostals as having a christological center and a pneumatological circumference.[4] Indeed, Pentecostal spirituality could be described as the experience of the presence of Jesus through the work of the Spirit. Daniel Castelo similarly comments:

> [T]he religious affections have their origin in the person of Christ and are actualized by the activity of the Spirit. One cannot aspire to the religious affections by one's own means and works, for these affections require the activity of the Holy Spirit to render them operative in the believer. These affections are

---

Charles Parham, whose death is symbolic of the end of first generation Pentecostals. Lewis, "Reflections on a Hundred Years of Pentecostal Theology."

3. Hollenweger, *Pentecostals*, 551; Land, *Pentecostal Spirituality*, 47.

4. Land, *Pentecostal Spirituality*, 23.

grounded in Christ, for they are "dispositions in response to or
in imitation of Christ . . ."[5]

Central to Pentecostal worship and prayer is a dynamic understanding of how the Spirit makes Jesus' presence real for the church and the
believer. Thus, when a pastor or preacher makes a prophetic announcement "in the Spirit" saying, "Jesus is here," it is taken literally, for the congregation understands that Jesus' presence will bring salvation, healing,
and deliverance now through the Spirit.

Yet, how this experience of Jesus through the Spirit illumines the
Christology of early Pentecostals is not clearly articulated. Indeed, a dynamic understanding of the person and work of Christ is fundamental
for comprehending the theological framework of early Pentecostalism.
How then can one speak of a Christology in early Pentecostalism? On
the one hand, Pentecostalism inherited its basic christological understanding from the movements out of which it developed—Methodism,
the Holiness Movement, and American Revivalism, among others.[6] On
the other hand, it is important to realize that early Pentecostal thought
about the person and work of Jesus contains theological affirmations
that differ from those traditions, and that what distinguishes their
christological reflections is their pneumatological perspective.

The Pentecostal Christological Inheritance

Like all movements that grow out of prior traditions, Pentecostalism
developed within systems of thought with a defined christological
construct. By outlining this inheritance, it is possible to highlight the
distinctiveness of Pentecostal reflection on the person and work of
Jesus. There are two thinkers whose Christology shaped that of early
Pentecostalism: John Wesley and A. B. Simpson.[7]

5. Castelo, "Tarrying on the Lord, 37." Behind these words one can detect the influence of Jonathan Edwards and John Wesley, whom Castelo follows closely, though
clearly with a more pneumatological concern.

6. Donald Dayton provides the classical interpretation of Pentecostalism's theological foundations in his masterful account of the *Theological Roots of Pentecostalism*.

7. In contrast to Irving, one could easily trace the influence of Wesley and Simpson
on early Pentecostal thought. Concerning the Wesleyan connection, Steven Land goes
as far as naming him Pentecostalism's grandfather. Land, *Pentecostal Spirituality*, 35.
In fact Wesley's influence on Pentecostalism is so richly documented in significant
Pentecostal scholarly works that it has become commonplace to acknowledge it. See

Behind the Pentecostal movements of the early nineteenth century, one can find the influence of John Wesley's Methodism and his Christology of sanctification or perfection. Wesley's governing principle for his Methodist program, Christian perfection, was clearly christocentric; indeed, for Wesley soteriology and Christology were inseparable.[8] Wesley understood that there were two basic steps in the soteriological process: first, on account of Christ's redemptive death on the cross we are pardoned from sin (justified by faith through grace); second, though saved by grace, we are responsible in grace for working out our salvation. In other words, God not only justifies but also imparts righteousness through sanctification. Thus, the Christian life consists in an active participation in the quest for Christian perfection or holiness.

Wesley's Christology, then, can be described as a Christology of sanctification, for he considered Jesus' divine and human natures from the standpoint of the righteousness that is imputed to the believer on account of Jesus' righteousness. Wesley distinguished the "divine righteousness" in Jesus from his "human righteousness."[9] According to Wesley, Jesus' "divine righteousness" refers to his "immutable holiness," which he shares with God the Father and the Spirit, whereas his "human righteousness" comprises his internal and exterior purity present in his earthly life. Wesley equated Jesus' internal human righteousness with

> the image of God, stamped on every power and faculty of his soul. It is a copy of his divine righteousness, as far as it can be imparted to a human spirit. It is a transcript of the divine purity,

Dayton, *Theological Roots of Pentecostalism*; Faupel, *Everlasting Gospel*; Synan, *Holiness-Pentecostal Tradition*; and Bevins, *Rediscovering John Wesley*. With regards to Simpson, Gary B. McGee comments, "While Simpson did not become a Pentecostal himself, his modeling of the 'higher life' in Christ, burden for missions, prayer for the sick, and anticipation of 'signs and wonders' in ministry blazed the way for many who became Pentecostals . . . Not surprisingly, the 'Fourfold Gospel' and other Alliance doctrines reappear in the Assemblies' 'Statement of Fundamental Truths' with some modifications. Simpson's Missionary Training Institute served as the model for Assemblies of God schools such as Glad Tidings Bible Institute (Bethany College), Central Bible Institute (Central Bible College), and Southern California Bible School (Southern California College). Among the earliest Council missionaries who attended Bible institutes, the largest number were trained at Simpson's Institute in Nyack, New York." McGee, "All for Jesus."

8. Deschner, *Wesley's Christology*, 14.

9. Wesley, "The Lord Our Righteousness," sermon preached November 24, 1765, in *Works of John Wesley* (hereafter abbreviated *WJW*) 5:236.

the divine justice, mercy, and truth. It includes love, reverence, resignation to his Father; humility, meekness, gentleness; love to lost mankind, and every other holy and heavenly temper; and all these in the highest degree, without any defect, or mixture of unholiness.[10]

With regard to Jesus' exterior human righteousness, Wesley contended that not only did Jesus not sin, but "all he acted and spoke was exactly right in every circumstance": a complete obedience and submission to God's will.[11] This "human righteousness" and "divine righteousness" in Jesus come together soteriologically (for Wesley considered the two as intrinsically linked[12]) on the cross. For through his death, the righteousness of Jesus is imputed onto us, as well as the ability to live in righteousness; the way of Jesus becomes the way to Christian perfection.

Central to Christian perfection is the notion of becoming like Christ. Donald Dayton explains it like this: "When Wesley wished to describe 'one that is perfect' he often spoke first of 'one in whom is the mind which was in Christ and who so walketh as He walked.'"[13] Christ not only provides the basis for our salvation and initial sanctification but also the pattern for our continued sanctification.[14] Logically, then, Wesley dedicated a great portion of his sermons to the Sermon on the Mount, where Jesus calls his disciples to a life of perfection (Matt 5:48) and where his ethics for the kingdom are explained as being of a higher degree of righteousness in comparison to the Mosaic Law.[15] Thus, Christian perfection is equated to "Christ-likeness," and Christo-praxis becomes central for living out a life of sanctification.

10. Ibid.

11. Ibid., 237.

12. Ibid.

13. Dayton, *Theological Roots*, 43–44.

14. It seems here that Wesley was sympathetic to the Eastern christological tradition, which focused on the incarnation and emphasized human beings partaking of the divine nature (*theosis*/deification). See Maddox, *Responsible Grace*, 114–15.

15. Dayton makes this observation: "Fourteen of the basic forty-four sermons of Wesley—along with the *Explanatory Notes on the New Testament*, the doctrinal standard of Methodism—are devoted to an exposition of the Sermon on the Mount and follow immediately upon the Sermons on the New Birth." Dayton, *Theological Roots*, 58.

With this in mind, one could label Wesley's reflection on the person and work of Jesus as a "mimetic Christology."[16] In other words, Wesley was more concerned with the imitation of Christ than with mere speculation about the nature of his person.[17] Paradigmatically, Jesus walked before us and traced the way for us to follow; the Gospels provide the life of Christ as the example of the Christian life.

A second influence on early Pentecostal Christology is the Christology of the Full Gospel.[18] The founder of the Christian and Missionary Alliance, A. B. Simpson, expounded a fourfold model of "Christ Our Savior, Sanctifier, Healer, and Coming King."[19] The CMA's christocentric mission can be seen in the following quotation:

> Pre-eminently we are witnesses for Christ. We are glad to testify to Him before we speak of His blessings or gifts to men. It is Christ as a Person, as a living reality, as the supreme fact of history and Life, Jesus Himself, who is the theme of our testimony . . . Above everything else this is a Christ movement. If we are saved it is Christ who saves us. If we are sanctified it is Christ who is made unto us sanctification. If we are healed it is because His life is in us. And the hope of the future is not the glory he is to reveal, but the return of the King himself, our beloved and our Friend.[20]

16. Commenting on the prospect of a Christology of mimesis, Jon M. Ruthven considers that Pentecostal preachers regularly express "their intuitive (or perhaps simply, biblical) insight that 'everything Jesus did we should do, because he was empowered by the same Holy Ghost we have'—in other words, a Christology of *mimesis*. Indeed, we would argue, something like this expression can be demonstrated as a key NT theme." Ruthven, "Jesus as Rabbi."

17. In his study of Wesley's theology, Howard A. Slaaté, has this to say about the nature of Wesley's Christology: "Though Wesley saw the two aspects of Christ as metaphysically basic and the incarnation as central to the God and man relationship, he did not stress this abstractly so much as he emphasized the mystery and eventfulness of God-in-Christ." Slaaté, *Purview of Wesley's Theology*, 49.

18. According to Dayton, the "logic of Pentecostal theology" can be summarized by this christocentric fourfold pattern of the "full gospel"—Christ is our Savior, Healer, Baptizer, and Soon-Coming King. Dayton notes, however, that Pentecostals shift from Jesus the Sanctifier to Jesus the Baptizer, which became the quintessential doctrine of Pentecostalism. Dayton, *Theological Roots*, 21.

19. Simpson, *Four-Fold Gospel*. Though this work was published clearly after the birth of Pentecostalism, the preface to the book correctly explains that the Fourfold Gospel was the overriding theme that characterized Simpson's preaching and teaching since the early days of his ministry.

20. Pardington, *Twenty-Five Wonderful Years*, 48–49.

More significant, however, is the relationship that Simpson established between the earthly Jesus and the Holy Spirit. Simpson clearly understood Christology from a kenotic perspective, for he explained that Jesus was completely dependent on the Spirit throughout his ministry. Simpson put it like this:

> [Jesus] was truly the eternal God, very God, of very God. But when He came down from yonder heights of glory *He suspended the direct operation of His own independent power and became voluntarily dependent upon the power of God through the Holy Ghost.*.. He purposely took His place side by side with us, heeding equally with the humblest disciple the constant power of God to sustain Him in all His work... And so He went through life in the position of dependence, that He might be our public example and teach us that we too have the same secret of strength and power that He possessed, and that as surely as He overcame through the Holy Ghost, so may we.[21]

In another book, Simpson made this revealing comment:

> [B]ut [Jesus] was baptized of the Spirit thirty years later on the banks of the Jordan; and this made all the difference which we trace between His quiet years at Nazareth and His public ministry in Galilee and Judea. *From that time there were two persons united in the ministry of Jesus of Nazareth. The Holy Ghost, as a Divine person, was united with the person of Jesus Christ*, and was the source of His power and the inspiration of His teaching; and He constantly represented Himself as speaking the words and doing the works which the Spirit in Him prompted.[22]

Significantly, Simpson here came close to a Spirit-Christology, for he understood the Spirit as intrinsically united to the person of Jesus in his ministry. Just before this excerpt, Simpson acknowledged that "Jesus was born of the Spirit in Bethlehem."[23] Yet, he introduced the above segment using the conjunction "but." Thus, though Simpson understood the birth of Jesus to have occurred through the power of the Spirit, he would say that it was not until his baptism that Jesus became united to the Spirit in such a way that the Spirit was the source of his power to do miracles and the inspiration behind his teaching.

21. Simpson, *Holy Spirit*, 25; emphasis added.

22. Simpson, *Walking in the Spirit*, 7–8; emphasis added.

23. Ibid., 7.

Although Simpson made these remarks without completely exploring what he meant, a few observations can be gleaned from them. First, it can readily be seen that Simpson ascribed to a Trinitarian understanding of God, and understood Jesus himself as possessing personal divinity, not merely equating the Spirit to the divine presence in him.[24] Thus, if one were to flesh out Simpson's seminal comments on the relation between Jesus and the Spirit, one could very well label it a conservative Spirit-Christology in the making. For although he posited an almost total submission of Jesus to the Spirit in his healings and teaching ministry, Simpson nonetheless considered Jesus' divinity as already present at his incarnation, and references his pre-existence.

Significantly, Simpson elaborated his incipient Spirit-Christology in a way that is similar to Wesley's Christology, though clearly Simpson's emphasis is on the activity of the Spirit, whereas for Wesley Jesus' humanity (his ability to live a life of perfection) is more significant. One might consider, however, that these approaches represent two sides of the same coin. On the one hand, Wesley's soteriological concern emphasized Jesus' righteous humanity; on the other hand, Simpson's pneumatological orientation focused on his dependence on the Spirit for his mission.

Christological Method in Early Pentecostal Theology

With Pentecostalism's christological inheritance in mind, what is the methodological overlap between Wesley and Simpson's main christological interests and that of early Pentecostal thinkers? Early Pentecostals' apparent disinterest in doing formal (or scholastic) Christology grows out of the pursuit for a practical understanding of doctrine and theology. Thus, it is not that early Pentecostals failed to work out their understanding on the person and work of Jesus, but rather that they went about it in a different manner from other faith traditions.[25]

24. Simpson made this evident when he wrote, "His relation to the second person of the Godhead is very clearly revealed; it was He who ministered in His incarnation, and through whom He became the Son of Man as well as the Son of God. It was He who personally united Himself with the person of Christ, and became the power of all His miracles and teachings." Ibid., 24.

25. Although anti-intellectualism was present in early Pentecostalism, several scholars argue that it is not enough simply to label the lack of academic publication as proof. For in developing their understanding of their doctrine at a popular or ecclesial level, they were in fact doing theology, albeit not in a traditional sense. Comparing it to the fundamentalist approach of the day, Harvey Cox says this about the way early

First, it is worth noting that admittedly Wesley did not care for abstract philosophical speculation when it came to Christology. As John Deschner comments, "This does not mean that he has no Christology; it means that he has an eye for what is useful for plain people, and a respect for the mysteries of faith."[26] Similarly, when considering the writings of early Pentecostals, one needs to take note of their audience and intent. The majority of their writings are directed to the church, at a popular level. For the most part, they did not produce theological treatises on specific themes. However, even if their approach is at variance with more rigorous academic works, their writings do embark on theological discussion in ways that are significantly unique and innovative.

Second, in order to think more critically about early Pentecostals' approach to doing Christology, it will prove useful to look briefly at John Wesley's experiential approach to Scripture, which is very much in line with the Pentecostal appropriation of the biblical text. Describing his theological method, Thomas A. Langford states, "Wesley understood theology to be intimately related to Christian living and the proclamation of Christian faith. Theology is actualized in authentic living and true proclamation."[27] This certainly entails a praxiological approach to theology: a method where the Christian life and witness take priority over pure systematic articulation. As Langford states, Wesley's "theological mode of operation was developed over time and was organic to his personal experience and his mission. His way of doing theology evolved as his natural way of approaching and dealing with theological issues."[28] As a result of Wesley's "method" we find no systematic treatment of theology penned by his hand. Instead, we have a large collection of letters he wrote in response to specific questions addressed to him, sermons

---

Pentecostals went about doing theology: "The difference is that while the beliefs of the fundamentalists, and of many other religious groups, are enshrined in formal theological systems, those of pentecostalism are imbedded in testimonies, ecstatic speech, and bodily movement. But it *is* a theology, a full-blown religious cosmos, an intricate system of symbols that respond to the perennial questions of human meaning and value. The difference is that, historically, Pentecostals have felt more at home singing their theology, or putting it in pamphlets for distribution on streets corners. Only recently have they begun writing books about it." Cox, *Fire from Heaven*, 15. See also Jacobsen, *Thinking in the Spirit*.

26. Deschner, Wesley's Christology, 14.

27. Langford, "John Wesley and Theological Method," 35.

28. Ibid., 36.

he preached concerning Christian living, and essays he composed out of the need to clarify positions he briefly mentioned in the course of his preaching and teaching ministry.

As with Wesley, the Christian experience of the presence of God is a focal point of Pentecostal reflection. By "experience" here I mean "the experience of faith that has been ignited by the Word of God and the Holy Spirit."[29] Thus, what is meant is not a mere detached episode where a person or a community feels goose bumps or the hair on the back of the neck rise—in other words, no psychological or purely emotional act of experiencing. Here, Land provides a helpful understanding of how the Pentecostal experience informs our theological understanding: "Experience of the Spirit . . . drives toward and requires this integration of belief, affections and practice which is at once the definition of spirituality and of the theological task."[30] For Pentecostals, then, spirituality is not diametrically opposed to the act of theologizing; indeed, it is an integral part of it as the two go hand in hand.[31]

Even today, when a Pentecostal approaches the Scriptures she or he does so with the preconceived notion that her or his experience of God through the Spirit is a perfectly suitable standpoint from which to engage not only with what the text means but more significantly with what it means today for her or him as an individual and for the worshipping community. A Pentecostal does not leave his or her spirituality at the door in order to recover the meaning of the biblical text objectively.

---

29. Arrington, "Use of the Bible," 106.

30. Land, *Pentecostal Spirituality*, 41.

31. Ironically, even today many Pentecostal pastors and preachers would at first glance oppose this line of thinking on the basis that an academic approach to the Bible cannot be reconciled with a prayerful one. Thus, arguing from the opposite end of the issue, they would insist that theologizing has no place within the realm of the Spirit. As someone who has remained active in church ministry throughout my academic pilgrimage, I have found the Society of Pentecostal Studies a prime example of where the two disciplines (theology and spirituality) are viewed as complementary, and indeed, inseparable. The reality is that pitting the two over against each other creates a false dichotomy that historically is not the norm but the exception. Considering the place for a "spiritual theology" Simon Chan pointedly writes, "Thinking about God and praying to God are not two discrete acts which we must somehow try to bring together by some mechanical bridge called 'spiritual application'; rather, they are ultimately a single act of relating to God. If Pentecostals in the early twenty-first century are to recover the heart of the movement in the first ten years, they need to develop a Pentecostal spiritual theology." Chan, *Pentecostal Theology*, 31–32.

Instead, it is precisely the experience of God through the Spirit that gives Pentecostals their distinctive understanding and thus witness to the greater ecclesial community.[32]

Terry Cross recently voiced Pentecostalism's unique approach to interpreting Scripture:

> As a Pentecostal interpreter of the text of Scripture, I believe that it is crucial to have all of the tools of scholarship in my intellectual toolbox as I do the work of interpreting Scripture. I must also have the Spirit's guidance to read the text. Moreover, I believe that in some way my *experience of God* will inform my reading of Scripture—indeed, it *must inform* that reading or the text becomes just another ancient text alongside Cicero or Plato or Seneca. It is the Spirit of God who breathed into life the Scriptures through the writing of the authors and it is that same Spirit who allows me to experience the God of Scripture in my daily life *and* in my work at interpreting the text.[33]

Although it is not fair to say that early Pentecostals would have expressed their theological convictions in this way, it is not at all misleading to affirm that Cross' articulation of his own approach to Scripture accurately and representatively speaks of the appeal to experience that Pentecostalism has had from its origins.

Indeed, as Kenneth J. Archer demonstrates in his study of Pentecostal hermeneutics, Pentecostal reflection has always focused on the dialogical relationship between Spirit, Scripture, and community.[34] Concerning early Pentecostal hermeneutics Archer states:

> Pentecostals found biblical parallels with their life experiences and would incorporate these into their testimonies. This rein-

32. Various terms have been used to name the peculiar appeal to experience that Pentecostals include in their hermeneutical method. In describing early Pentecostal's interpretative ethos, Donald Dayton refers to it as a "subjectivizing hermeneutic," in that they take the narrative of the reception of the Spirit in Acts 2 as experientially normative. Dayton, *Theological Roots*, 24. Building on Max Weber's Charismatic model, Margaret Paloma refers to the Pentecostal reliance on experience as "affective action," in order to stress that for Pentecostals, "sentiment, rather than rationality, is the basis for action." For a critical and constructive approach to Pentecostal "experiencing," see Althouse, "Toward a Theological Understanding," 399–411; Paloma quotation from ibid., 401.

33. Cross, "Review of Ben Witherington," 6.

34. Archer, *Pentecostal Hermeneutic*, ix.

forced the Pentecostal story. Hence, Pentecostals did not see a difference between how God worked in biblical times and how God worked in the present. In addition, they did not recognize any difference in perceived reality due to the changing of time or culture. People have always had similar experiences. Thus, they saw their experiences similar to Bible times. This outlook reiterated the easy accessibility and immediacy of the meaning of Scripture for their Pentecostal community.[35]

In light of this comment, one can consider early Pentecostals' reflection of Jesus to be closely connected with their daily experience of him through the Spirit.

Thinking of Jesus in the Spirit

Early Pentecostal reflection is notable particularly for its characteristic pneumatological orientation. It is perhaps not surprising that a movement spawned from the quest to restore the early church's pneumatic origins would focus on developing its central motif of the baptism in the Holy Spirit at the expense of other doctrinal concerns. Yet, the phrase "thinking in the Spirit" does not mean "thinking about the Spirit" or even "thinking with a pneumatological orientation." For even before the birth of Pentecostalism there was much concern regarding the person, nature, and purpose of the Holy Spirit. Moreover, in the last century various theologies have developed a thoroughly pneumatological focus.

French L. Arrington assists in understanding the dynamics of thinking in the Spirit. He puts it like this:

> A fundamental principle of Pentecostal hermeneutics is: Scripture given by the Holy Spirit must be mediated interpretively by the Holy Spirit. The illumination of the interpreter by the Holy Spirit is a vital part in elucidating the contemporary meaning of the biblical text. So in the interpretative process the Holy Spirit has a broader role than simply taking the things of the incarnate Christ and declaring them to us (John 16:14).[36]

In fact, for early Pentecostals it would be audacious to think that one could rightly and fully interpret the text without the assistance of the

35. Ibid., 122.
36. Arrington, "Use of the Bible," 104.

Holy Spirit. Instead it is always only through and by the Spirit that one can pick up this ancient text and find in it meaning that is relevant for today's world. Arrington states forcefully:

> [T]he Holy Spirit overcomes the distance by serving as the common context and bridging the temporal and cultural distance between the original author and the modern interpreter. Put differently, the Spirit establishes a continuum between the written word of the past and the same word in the present, thereby illuminating what the ancient author's words mean to us living in the twentieth century and how they speak to us today. Through the Holy Spirit the Word of God becomes alive and speaks to our present situation with new possibilities for personal and social transformation.[37]

What becomes significant in the Pentecostal reflection of Jesus, then, is the importance of the working of the Spirit both in the life of Jesus (as recorded in the biblical text) and also in our experiential understanding of Jesus' continued work in our lives today through his Spirit. Early Pentecostals keenly grasped this principle, for the essence of their thinking—the Fivefold Gospel—presents an understanding of Jesus that is thoroughly driven by a pneumatic orientation. For them Jesus is Savior, Healer, Sanctifier, Baptizer, and Soon-Coming King precisely because of the continued activity of the Spirit. Early Pentecostal Christology does not focus on the abstract understanding of how Jesus is God and man simultaneously, or on how that ministry can best be grasped today, although certainly early Pentecostals believed Jesus to be fully God and man. Instead, the principal focus of early Pentecostal Christology was the work of Jesus in his earthly life and his continued ministry today through the power of the Spirit.

Jesus and the Fivefold Gospel: Recovering Early Pentecostal Christology

Guided by the principles developed in the previous sections, I now systematize early Pentecostal Christology by integrating the most significant christological themes that appear in its early writings to the foundational Fivefold model. Thus, I organize early Pentecostal reflec-

---

37. Ibid.

tion on Jesus' person and work using the categories of Jesus Christ the Savior, Sanctifier, Baptizer, Healer, and Soon-Coming King.

Throughout this descriptive outline, it is my aim to show that early Pentecostal Christology can more accurately be developed, in true accord with its heritage, by following the paradigm of Spirit-Christology instead of the conventional two-natures Chalcedonian model that has traditionally been used in previous attempts at a Pentecostal systematic theology.[38] Indeed, after analyzing early Pentecostal reflection on Jesus, it will become evident that Spirit-Christology is more akin to their christological affirmations, and therefore provides a better paradigm for Pentecostal Christology.

Jesus Christ the Savior

Considering the large corpus of early Pentecostal writings, it would be nearly impossible to synthesize their reflection on the person and work of Jesus. However, because of the rich descriptive reflection produced by early Pentecostals, it is possible to organize their understanding of Jesus as Savior by analyzing the titles, metaphors, and theological motifs toward which their thought gravitated. The main titles, metaphors, and motifs used to speak of Jesus' saving work were: Son of God, Lamb of God, Jesus' blood, and the cross.[39]

In the first issue of one of the earliest Pentecostal periodicals, *The Apostolic Faith*, William J. Seymour stated that there are four key benefits made available for us through the atoning death of Jesus: 1) forgiveness of sins, 2) sanctification, 3) healing, and 4) the baptism with the Holy

---

38. Arguably, Pentecostals have yet to produce a systematic theology in the strict sense of the term, because they fail to fully thread a central concept through the classical theological themes in order to produce a tightly woven system of thought. However, such an understanding of systematic theology is a more recent development; various prominent theologians have produced theological works that also do not comply with this definition. The Pentecostal works I have in mind are doctrinal statements and systematic theologies published by a specific denomination (or one of its prominent theologians) representative of a movement's thinking. These include: Pearlman, *Knowing the Doctrines*; Williams, *Systematic Theology*; Duffield and Van Cleave, eds., *Foundations of Pentecostal Theology*; Higgins et al., eds., *Introduction to Theology*; Horton, ed., *Systematic Theology*; and Arrington, *Christian Doctrine*.

39. These christological themes comes together in a short reflection by William J. Seymour entitled "The Way into the Holiest." He comments that when a sinner attempts to come to God justification is needed and this is made possible through Jesus, "the Lamb without blemish" who as "the Son of God, cleanses him from all sin."

Spirit.[40] Yet, although Pentecostal reflection would expound largely on the last three, the first is primary. First and foremost, early Pentecostal reflection considered Jesus as the Savior of the sinner and the world.

The editor of the very popular early Pentecostal periodical *The Bridegroom's Messenger*, Gaston B. Cashwell (a Methodist minister who later joined a Holiness church), summarized the salvific work of Jesus on the cross like this:

> The last words of our Lord Jesus on the cross were, "It is finished." In the mind of God and in his perfect provision for fallen humanity, Jesus as the Lamb slain from the foundation of the world and his precious blood has always been efficacious for the remission of our sins and from the cleansing from all our iniquities... The finished work of Christ covers every need of suffering humanity. It provides perfect redemption from the curse of sin for body, mind and spirit.[41]

Cashwell went on to explain that the fuller understanding of Christ's redemptive work includes the remission of sin, but also the cleansing of our iniquities and healing for our bodies. So when early Pentecostals referred to Jesus as their Savior, what they had in mind was a more holistic view of salvation: a Savior who makes provision for all the needs of human beings whether spiritual, emotional, or physical.

Seeking to explain who Jesus is in relation to humanity, early Pentecostal writers gave Scriptural accounts of Jesus as Savior. Sam C. Perry, for example, stated, "Jesus, the Son of God, the Redeemer, comes to rescue and provide glorious deliverance for poor fallen humanity."[42] Then, he continued to thread the theme of Jesus as Savior through various Scripture references. Significantly, Perry made some interesting remarks concerning the person of Jesus that aimed to establish who Jesus is as our Savior. Perry emphatically commented, "Jesus is not the Savior because of the fact that he is God's Son or omnipresent or omnipotent or omniscient, but because he is 'the slain lamb' for our sins, our Mediator between God and man; 'the propitiation for our sins and the sins of the

---

40. Seymour, "Precious Atonement," 2.

41. Cashwell, "Our Lord's Finished Work."

42. Perry, "Bloodless Salvation?"

whole world.'"[43] Thus, although Jesus is God's Son, he became our Savior in eternity when he was appointed "the slain lamb of Calvary."

The metaphor of the Lamb of God is further linked to the concept of the perfect humanity of Jesus and became a persistent theme in early Pentecostal writings. The purity of Jesus' blood shed on the cross is what accounts for its power to save and deliver from sin. Commenting on Jesus as the High Priest, Perry wrote:

> [Jesus] is holy, harmless, undefiled, separate from sinners, and made higher than the heavens, who did no sin, neither was guile found in his mouth. He was the spotless Lamb of God, there was no blemish in Him and no defilement, if there had been He could not have been the Savior of the world. He could neither have atoned for the sins of the people nor have washed away the depravity of the human heart.[44]

Referring to the Passover Lamb of Exodus as a type of Christ in the Old Testament, Seymour stated three times that Jesus' perfect body was given on the cross as a sacrifice.[45] Later in the same issue, there is a short reflection entitled "The Spotless Lamb of God," where the author (presumably Seymour, editor and main contributor of the periodical) elaborated further:

> [I]f His precious blood had not flowed from a Lamb without blemish and without spot, but had carnality and corruption from self, from the manger to the cross, then it is only the blood of a martyr, and its atoning merits are void. If there is any point in the Gospel which is fundamentally absolute, it is the purity of the person of Jesus Christ, God's Son.[46]

What became fundamental to early Pentecostal understanding of the person and work of Jesus is the absolute purity of his humanity.

Significantly, then, early Pentecostal Christology departed from the humanity of Jesus, for it is in his human manifestation as the Son of God that his redemptive work on behalf of humanity was achieved. To

43. Ibid.

44. Other articles that share the same insistence on the absolute purity of Jesus Christ and focus on the theme of the blood of Jesus include: Perry, "Blood of Jesus"; idem, "Bloodless Salvation?"; Tomlinson, "Saved by the Blood"; and idem, "Jesus Our Savior."

45. Seymour, "Salvation and Healing."

46. Seymour, "Spotless Lamb of God."

begin with, Jesus became incarnate in order to give his life as a ransom for the whole human race. The reason for the incarnation is further expressed as a willful decision on the part of the Son. Joseph Tunmore explained:

> Jesus, away back in eternity, before anything was created, promised the Father that when man fell He would come down to the earth and take upon Himself our humanity; that He would take man's place and do what man failed to do. He told His father He would give Himself a ransom for the whole human race.[47]

Tunmore later commented that what man failed to do was defeat Satan in his own territory:

> When God made and created this earth He never intended it to be ruled by a disembodied spirit [Satan], so when Jesus came, He came as a man, took upon Himself our humanity. He redeemed the world as a Man, He conquered the devil as a man, and when he went back to glory He was different than when He came. He was always the Eternal Son of God, but when He took upon Himself our flesh and went back again He was not only the Eternal Son of God, but was a glorified human being, and He is sitting on the throne of the Father this afternoon a glorified Man.[48]

Thus, the earthly mission of Jesus, the human Son of God, was to conquer the devil and redeem humanity, and it was essential for this task that he accomplish it as a man.

The victory over the devil had to take place in the spiritual sphere, where the battle had been lost at the beginning in the Garden of Eden. As a man, Jesus came to overcome Satan by living a life without blemish and then offering it to God as a perfect sacrificial offering. For this, Jesus "had to be the son of a virgin" and live out his life in complete obedience to the Father.[49] Yet, the only possible way to achieve this would be through the agency of the Holy Spirit. From the beginning of his life and until his return to the Father, the Son would depend on the Spirit in order to achieve the salvation of humanity; living a spotless/perfect

---

47. Tunmore, "Why Jesus Took Our Humanity," 9.

48. Ibid., 10.

49. Jamieson, "Virgin Birth," 8. See also, Bayerhaus, "Birth of Christ."

life and offering it to God at death would only be possible through the work of the Spirit.

In thinking about Jesus' person and work, early Pentecostals brought Christology and pneumatology together.[50] According to G. F. Taylor, "Jesus did His work through the power of the Spirit. He preached through the Spirit. He worked miracles through the Spirit of God. It was through the Spirit that he died on the cross and by the Spirit that He was raised from the dead."[51] In fact, the Holy Spirit made the incarnation itself possible.[52] Alexander A. Boddy[53] commented, "When God the Son stooped to take our nature, He was 'born of the Spirit.'"[54] Yet, the Spirit was not only responsible for the human existence of Jesus, but also the secret to his ability to live a perfect life before God in order to achieve redemption. Boddy recognized the activity of the Spirit in the earthly life of Jesus in this way:

> Born of the Spirit, [Jesus'] human life was lived out in His [the Spirit's] companionship and power. When the day came for His entering on His ministry of preaching and healing He was filled with the Spirit as He came up from His baptism in Jordan (John

50. Characteristic of this tendency, J. W. Welch states, "The Holy Spirit and Jesus never work separately." Welch, "Ministry of the Spirit."

51. Taylor, "Sunday School Lesson," 4–5.

52. Seymour went as far as to say that "Jesus' body was one without carnality" because "[i]t was a body that God prepared from heaven by the Holy Ghost and sent down into this world to be the bread of Life." In this sense, the activity of the Spirit in the humanity of Jesus would have begun even before his incarnation. Though clearly this comment is highly speculative and without Scriptural support, it is nonetheless significant because it highlights the relation between the Son and the Spirit even in the pre-existent state of Jesus. Seymour, "Virtue in the Perfect Body."

53. I am aware that A. A. Boddy never actually left the Anglican Church, having always remained in holy orders. Moreover, although, his Charismatic credentials cannot be denied, it must be stated that he was active in the Pentecostal movement in England and not the U.S. However, his influence upon the early Pentecostalism in the U.S. was such that a good number of articles appear in various Pentecostal periodicals published in the U.S. The inclusion of his articles here is due to the widespread acceptation that his writings had among Pentecostals. What is more, the fact that a significant Pentecostal periodical, *The Pentecostal Evangel* (the official publication of the AG), published it attests to a full agreement with his views, for otherwise it would not have passed through the editorial filters. See Bundy, "Boddy," 436–37.

54. Here Boddy is commenting on Luke 1:35: "The Holy Ghost shall come upon thee, and the power of the Highest shall overshadow thee, therefore also that Holy Thing which shall be born of thee shall be called the Son of the highest." Boddy, "Holy Ghost for Us."

1:32–33; Matt 3:11–16). Day by day in His humanity we believe
that He maintained His Spirit power by prayer and unbroken
communion with His Father. Thus, He lived the perfect life, although He was human and willing to be empty for the time of
divine attributes.[55]

Now, Boddy was careful to indicate that Jesus never "ceased to be the
eternal Word," that at all times he was "Very God of Very God."[56] Yet, he
remarked, "His humanity veiled completely His deity."[57] By this Boddy
meant that at no time did Jesus exercise his divine powers independently, but was always relying on the Spirit to accomplish his mission.

This idea about Jesus' dependence on the Spirit is not a well-docu-
mented christological theme, but it does appear in the earliest periodicals and occurs throughout the early phase of Pentecostalism.[58] In one
of the first publications of *The Church of God Evangel*, A. S. Worrell remarked vividly, "If it was a fearful sin to ascribe the works of Jesus done
in the power of the Holy Spirit to Satan, must it not be a horrible sin to
ascribe to Satan the works of the Spirit in those who are filled with His

55. Ibid.

56. Ibid.

57. Ibid.

58. For example, although S. D. L. Jenkins insists that Spirit-Christology is a better
paradigm for Pentecostal Christology, his documentary evidence is limited because
his study focuses solely on three early Pentecostal periodicals: *The Apostolic Faith*, *The
Bridegroom's Messenger*, and *The Church of God Evangel* (though he also cites examples
from A. S. Copley's works). With regard to *The Church of God Evangel* and early writers
belonging to the named denomination, Jenkins argues, "there is little reflection upon
the interaction of the Holy Spirit in the life of Jesus Christ." Jenkins, "Human Son of
God," 49. Though this might be true concerning this periodical and denomination,
Jenkins recognizes that first generation Pentecostal thinkers "exhibit the *initial inclination* to locate the work of the Spirit in the life and ministry of Jesus" (69) and, thus, seem
to move in a trajectory toward a Spirit-Christology—albeit not articulated in formal
theological categories, but existent in an incipient form. I would go further to say that
a fuller treatment of christological themes in early Pentecostal writings reveals more
than just an inclination toward Spirit-Christology, but a strong preference for such a
paradigm. In the end, Jenkins' lack of documentation is most likely due to his greater
goals of recovering the Spirit-Christology of Edward Irving as "an adequate theological
framework upon which to establish a Pentecostal, incarnational, Spirit-Christology"
(70), and bringing recent Pentecostal contributions to Christology into conversation
with contemporary Spirit-Christologies. Moreover, one must also realize that his efforts
are more ecumenically oriented, rather than simply directed toward the early phase of
Pentecostalism. For a more thorough documentation of early Pentecostalism's strong
support for Spirit-Christology, see Tennison, "Logic of the Spirit," 171–79.

Holy Presence?"[59] A similar statement was made by A. S. Copley, who insisted that Jesus was, from the time his baptism at the Jordan, guarded and guided by the Holy Spirit in such a way that the miracles he worked and the power with which he taught were in effect due to his compliance to the Spirit.[60]

What is even more significant for this part of the discussion is the relation of the Spirit to Jesus in allowing the Son to live a perfect life. For example, Tunmore made this provocative comment:

> Jesus Christ came down in order that He might bring back and restore the fellowship and communion with the divine. . . God made a body for himself and the Word was made flesh and dwelt among us. And the blessed, divine Spirit entered into that body and sanctified it and enabled the Lord Jesus Christ in His humanity to go through this world, to resist every temptation, to give Himself a ransom for the sins of the whole world. He died on Calvary and was resurrected by the same divine Holy Spirit and was exalted to the right hand of God the Father.[61]

This idea of the Spirit enabling Jesus to live a perfect life is not rare in early Pentecostal thought; it is a persistent theme. In a sermon on the Holy Spirit, evangelist A. E. Stuernagel declared,

> The Holy Spirit never abode in the heart of anyone until He came in the form of a dove upon the head of our precious Redeemer as he stood in the waters of the Jordan. Jesus was the first one who was qualified to receive into His heart the Holy Spirit as an abiding Presence. He came as the Dove of Peace because in Jesus there was no sin or carnality. He was pure as a sunbeam, spotless as the driven snow. . . Then when the Lord had finished His ministry and had developed *a perfect character thru the Divine Spirit*, he went home to God. He had borne fruit in the finished work of Calvary, and now that work was accepted and He took the place of supreme authority at God's right hand.[62]

In a Sunday School lesson touching on Jesus' temptation, G. F. Taylor commented that "Jesus needed the Holy Spirit to enable Him to do

---

59. Worrell, "Crisis Now On," 4.

60. Copley, *Liberty of the Sons of God*, 36. Copley makes similar comments in two other articles: "Power from on High, II" and "Prayer of the Just."

61. Tunmore, "Holy Spirit," 5.

62. Stuernagel, "Pentecost," 2.

His work," and later suggested that "the Son of God was not beyond temptation."[63] Taylor's main concern in the article, although not explicitly stated in this part of the discussion, was the agency of the Spirit in assisting Jesus to defeat the devil's temptations.

Two more examples that relate to the Spirit's involvement in Jesus' learned obedience are found in early editions of *The Bridegroom's Messenger*. A. S. Copley insisted that "many times His (Jesus') own mind would have acted, and yet he learned obedience by letting the Spirit move."[64] Again, Copley cited Hebrews 5:8 ("Though being a Son, He learned obedience from the things which he suffered") and commented, "but this was after He was anointed with the Spirit."[65] In this way, Copley also linked the obedience of Jesus to the work of the Spirit.

What becomes evident in these examples is how Jesus was exclusively dependent upon the Spirit to continue to live in the sanctified ways with which he began his life.[66] In his daily living, Jesus needed the Spirit to overcome every temptation as a man, so that the sacrifice of his life might be offered in complete purity. After affirming that "the Holy Spirit was the power of the personal life of Jesus," indeed the very "root of his personal life," Tunmore summarized his thoughts by presenting Jesus as the best example for living a sanctified life:

> Born of the virgin Mary He walked in obedience to His parents. Because of His obedience He was baptized with the Holy Ghost, and He received a fuller measure or a fuller revelation of the Holy Spirit in His life. The Scriptures tell us that Jesus learned obedience through suffering, and so *there was a sense in which in His humanity the Lord Jesus had to go through things in order to receive and take the titles as the Christ of our salvation.*[67]

Thus, Jesus became the Captain of our salvation on account of his complete dependence on the Spirit on his way to Calvary. He lived and died as a man, but a man guided by the power of the Holy Spirit. During his

63. Taylor, "Sunday School Lesson," 5.

64. Copley, "Power from on High, I."

65. Copley, "Why We Need the Baptism."

66. Seymour puts it like this: "Jesus was the Son of God and born of the Holy Ghost and filled with the Holy Ghost from His mother's womb; but the baptism of the Holy Ghost came upon *His sanctified humanity* at the Jordan. In His humanity, He needed the Third person of the Trinity to do His work." Seymour, "Jesus' First Sermon."

67. Tunmore, "Holy Spirit," 6.

earthly existence, Jesus relinquished his divine powers and relied on the Spirit in order to become God's perfect and spotless sacrificial Lamb.

Yet, the Spirit's agency did not end with the death of Jesus on the cross. For at the time of his death, when his body was offered to God as a sacrifice for the redemption of humanity, the Spirit was also the active agent that accomplished this task. "We are told it was under the power of this eternal Spirit that on the cross He offered Himself without spot to God, and by the Holy Spirit He was raised from the dead (Heb 9:14; Rom 8:11)."[68] What is more, according to E. M. Stanton, it is the Holy Spirit who "makes the atonement of Christ effectual."[69] Such is the significance of the work of the Spirit that Stanton went so far as to say that "without His presence and power the work of Jesus could not avail anything."[70] Thus, it is in and through the Spirit that Jesus' sacrifice is both made and offered unto God. In this respect, one has to conclude that a pneumatological orientation is needed in order to flesh out what early Pentecostals believed concerning the salvific work of Jesus as God's Son.

Jesus Christ the Sanctifier[71]

Having laid a solid foundation concerning the relationship between the Spirit and Jesus, in his capacity as Savior, I turn now to cover briefly the rest of the categories of the Fivefold model of early Pentecostal Christology. In a very similar vein, Jesus' work as Sanctifier is tied to that of the Spirit. In effect, early Pentecostals posited such importance to the Holy Spirit's role in sanctification that, although the provision for sanctification is accomplished on and through the cross, it is nonetheless in and through the Spirit that they are applied to the church and the individual believer.

Returning to Seymour's four benefits of the atonement already mentioned above, the second blessing is sanctification through the blood of Jesus. Early Pentecostals made a connection with the ceremo-

68. Boddy, "Holy Ghost for Us." See also, Copley, "Pentecost in Type," 7; and Salter, "God's Man," 7.

69. Stanton, *Divine Indwelling*, 9.

70. Ibid., 10.

71. Since there is much overlap in the themes that follow and already in the previous section there has been some mention of the remaining four titles, the following sections will be shorter than the first.

nies and sacrifices described in the Old Testament. In them, they found types of Christ's sanctifying work. For example, the scapegoat and the slain goat of Leviticus 16 are identified as typifying Jesus.

> And this kind of sanctification that is obtained by the blood of Jesus subsequent to the taking away of all sins [*sic*]. Remember that in the description under the law the sins were to be sent away on the head of the scapegoat first, and then the remains of the slain goat were burned outside the camp that typifies the place where Jesus died that he might sanctify the people with His own blood.[72]

However, sanctification was understood by early Pentecostals as a work of cooperation between Jesus and the Spirit; Jesus provided the means for our sanctification and the Spirit makes it applicable to our lives. R. B. Beall made this point in a sermon:

> Since it is the Holy Ghost that convicts and the Holy Ghost that quickens and regenerates, it also is the Holy Ghost that sanctifies, or rather applies the blood that sanctifies, Rom. 15:16, 1 Cor. 6: 11. We see by these two passages that we are sanctified by the Spirit. But in Heb. 13:12, we read, "Wherefore Jesus also, that he might sanctify the people with his own blood," therefore, since the Holy Ghost is the executioner of the plan of salvation it is He that takes the blood and applies it to our hearts and sanctifies, of which He is a witness, Heb. 10: 14, 15.[73]

So although Pentecostals separated the baptism with the Spirit from sanctification, they did not deny the Spirit's participation in the latter. Rather, they distinguished between sanctification as a process that the believer enters at the time of conversion, and the reception or baptism with the Spirit as an endowment of power for witness.[74] Nonetheless, it is through the agency of the Spirit that the complete work of sanctification is applied or received. In a sermon, one evangelist described the joint activity of Jesus and the Spirit like this:

> Then the Holy Spirit as a fire also purifies. He did not come only as a life-giving, re-generating, empowering element, but as a mighty purifying agency. He came to those disciples purifying, separating and transforming. People say, 'Must I be sanctified to

72. Tomlinson, "Blood of Jesus," 1. See also, Cotnam, "Sanctification."

73. Beall, "Holy Spirit as a Person," 2.

74. Ibid., 3.

> receive the Holy Spirit?' You certainly must. You must be sanctified by the blood of Jesus Christ. Then the Holy Spirit as a mighty fire enters as an external antagonist to all of sin and self in you and thus purifies and delivers you from the dross of self. Talk about just speaking in tongues, if you get the real infilling of the Holy Spirit *you will first have a real sanctification thru [sic] the Divine Spirit*.[75]

Sanctification is both the work of Jesus and of the Spirit; it is as though Jesus begins the cleansing work and the Spirit, like a consuming fire, comes to finish the job that the Son started. The distinctive christological point made by this understanding of sanctification is perhaps better understood in connection with the work of Jesus as Baptizer in the Spirit, for it relates to the ongoing work of the Son in the power of the Spirit.

Jesus Christ the Baptizer

It is no surprise that early Pentecostals identified Jesus as the Holy Spirit Baptizer, for this is precisely the defining and lasting characteristic of Pentecostalism. One might say that this is the quintessential trait of what it means to be Pentecostal. The belief in the baptism with the Holy Spirit is *the* decisive feature that distinguishes the Pentecostal (inclusive of Charismatics and Neo-Charismatics) from the non-Pentecostal. What might be surprising, however, is that to speak of the baptism with the Holy Spirit early Pentecostals began by identifying Jesus as Spirit Baptized. There are plenty of authors who insisted that when Jesus was baptized in the Jordan he received the Spirit or was baptized in and with the Spirit.

For example, Seymour wrote, ". . . you have not the enduement [sic] of power until you are baptized with the Holy Spirit. Then you receive the baptism that Christ received on the banks of the Jordan. He had the fullness of the Godhead, but He had to be baptized for His great work."[76] Describing Jesus in his earthly existence, James Salter eloquently presented him as one clothed with the Spirit:

> Here was this Man clothed from heaven, divinely equipped, filled, charged, yes, surcharged with the great omnipotent Holy

75. Stuernagel, "Pentecost," 4–5.

76. Seymour, untitled article.

Ghost. He was equipped by One who would take Him through the remainder of His days on earth, held captive by the power from heaven that had met Him at the Jordan. He had no need to think what was coming next, for He had but to open His mouth and God's Word would flow through Him. He could stretch out His hand and God's power was with Him. He could tread with the dignity of the Son of God, clothed with the Holy Ghost.[77]

A correlation, then, is made between Jesus and his followers; for if he being divine needed the Spirit to do the work for which he was sent, how much more must his followers seek the Baptism with the Holy Spirit.[78] Jesus did not preach a single sermon or begin his mission in any way until the Holy Spirit had anointed him with power.[79] Only after being baptized with the Spirit after he ascended from the waters of baptism was he ready to do the work for which the Father had sent him.[80]

Significantly, though, it was only after his ascension to the right hand of the Father that Jesus was able to baptize believers with the Holy Spirit. During his earthly ministry, no one was baptized with the Holy Spirit, but upon his ascension he began to pour out his Spirit as evidence of his reign, authority, and position at the right hand of the Father.[81] This is why D. W. Kerr was able to declare emphatically that Jesus was behind all the activity of the Holy Spirit as recorded in the book of Acts.[82] Furthermore, he stated that Jesus' present office is that of baptizing believers with the Holy Spirit.

To pick up the thought that concluded the previous section, one might say that for early Pentecostals Christology was not concerned merely with the person and work of Jesus Christ in his pre-existent form and his earthly manifestation as known through the Scriptures; it was also concerned with his continued presence and workings through

---

77. Salter, "God's Man," 6.

78. Nelson, "Deliverance to the Captives," 6–7.

79. Ibid., 6.

80. The understanding that Jesus was baptized with the Holy Spirit during his baptism by John is expressed with clarity by the following authors, among others: Beall, "Holy Spirit as Person," 2; Copley, "Pentecost in Type," 8; idem, "Prayer of the Just," 2; idem, "Why We Need the Baptism"; King, "Passover to Pentecost"; McPherson, "Holy Spirit"; Salter, "God's Man," 4–5; Seymour, "Jesus' First Sermon"; W. W. Simpson, "Glory Given"; and Taylor, "Sunday School Lesson," 4.

81. Boddy, "Holy Ghost for Us."

82. Kerr, "Bible Evidence of the Baptism."

the Spirit in the church and the world. Kerr drove this point home as follows:

> There is no difference at all as to the manifestations of His [Jesus'] power during His earthly ministry and His heavenly ministry in casting out devils, healing the sick, raising the dead, cleansing the leper, causing the lame to walk, the blind to see, the deaf to hear and the dumb to speak. When Jesus Christ was upon the earth, He wrought miracles by the power of the Spirit, when He returned to heaven He continued to work by the same power. He is still in the same business as He was when He began. He has not changed His plan nor His program. He is doing the same things today as He did when He was upon this earth. He is doing the same thing today as He began to do on the Day of Pentecost.[83]

This is why from the beginning of the Pentecostal movement the slogan "Jesus Christ is the Same Yesterday, Today and Forever" (Heb 13:8) has been used widely to announce the fundamental theme of the Pentecostal understanding of the person and work of Jesus. It is not merely a catchy phrase or simply a fashionable idea; it articulates concisely and boldly the basic premise that Pentecostals have been announcing from the beginning of the past century.

Pentecostal faith is entirely christocentric in this respect, for devotion to Jesus by far surpasses its pneumatological interests. Pentecostals have consistently opted for a more dynamic understanding of the work of the Spirit, but always in the connection between Jesus and the Spirit. For instance, Tunmore spoke of the Spirit's manifestation in the life of believer's as being the very same "Spirit of the incarnate, crucified, resurrected, glorified Lord Jesus Christ."[84] In fact, he seemed to equate the Spirit with the presence of Jesus in our lives: "Let us by faith realize that the life-giving Spirit is down in our being, that the crucified, glorified, resurrected Lord Jesus Christ is down there."[85] Instead of a clear-cut identification of Jesus with the Spirit, however, it is better to understand this comment as elicit of the Spirit's role in manifesting Jesus' presence.

The Holy Spirit makes Jesus' presence real. For Pentecostals, this is not an abstract concept but a palpable experience that transforms ordi-

83. Ibid.
84. Tunmore, "Holy Spirit," 6.
85. Ibid., 6.

nary existence in a supernatural way. Jesus is present and experienced in the Pentecostal community by and through the Spirit. It is therefore puzzling why these dimensions of Pentecostal Christology are not expressly articulated in the various Pentecostal systematic theologies that have been produced thus far. Thus, we now explore the christological implications of Jesus activity as healer.

Jesus Christ the Healer

It would be unnecessary to try to list the most significant references to Jesus as Healer in the writings of early Pentecostalism, for these periodicals are a virtual depository of testimonies that document the healing power of Jesus Christ.[86] I have already provided ample references that Pentecostals believed the Spirit to be the active agent behind the miraculous signs performed by Jesus during his earthly ministry. What is significant for this study, however, is how the healing activity of Jesus is related to the work of the Spirit.

As Seymour noted with regard to the four benefits of the atonement, the provision for healing is made at the cross. We may cite numerous texts concerning the provision for healing in the atonement; these typically include a reflection on the Suffering Servant of Isaiah 53 as referring to Jesus.[87] With regard to the Spirit, some significant insights were made by an unidentified author in an article entitled "The Lord for the Body." To begin with, the risen life of Jesus is considered as "the physical source of our bodily strength."[88] Significantly, this is possible because Pentecostals affirm the resurrection of the Lord Jesus Christ as a physical fact. The author explained:

---

86. Many times these testimonies appear under a heading that announces in some way Jesus as the Healer; for example: Bridges, "Jesus Is Her Healer"; Childers, "Jesus the Only Healer"; Hicks, "Jesus the Great Healer"; Hutsell, "Jesus Is a Great Healer"; Ingram, "Jesus the Great Healer"; Lingerfelt, "Jesus Her Only Physician"; Mobley, "The Lord Is Her Healer"; and Weil, "The Lord Heals."

87. Among these some notable articles include: Barth, "Healing in the Atonement," 1–2; Doss, "Wonderful Healer"; Orwig, "Jesus as Saviour and Healer"; Perry, "Christ Our Healer and Health"; Sexton, "Divine Healing"; and Tomlinson, "Jesus Our Great Healer." Perhaps the best example of the early Pentecostal belief in Jesus as Healer is found in Bosworth's *Christ the Healer*.

88. "Lord for the Body," 10.

Now, this body of Christ is for our body. It is the head and body of our physical life, just as His Spirit is the source of our spiritual life; and just as we drew comfort and strength for our soul from communing with Him, so we may draw physical strength into our mortal frame by fellowship with His risen life.[89]

Healing evangelist F. F. Bosworth spoke of the Spirit's role based on his understanding explained here:

God's all-inclusive promise is to pour His Spirit upon all flesh during "the acceptable year of the Lord," which is the dispensation of the Holy Spirit. He comes as Christ's executive, to execute for us all the blessings of redemption—to bring to us "the earnest" or "firstfruits" of our *spiritual* and *physical* inheritance, until the last enemy, which is death, is destroyed, thus admitting us to our full inheritance.[90]

As with the other blessings, the Holy Spirit is seen as the active agent that brings about the healing provided for in the atonement. In this sense, Christ is the Healer, but the channel through which healing is appropriated is the Holy Spirit. Bosworth also connected healing to the life of the risen Christ as applied to us by the Holy Spirit:

In John 6:63, Jesus said, "It is the Spirit that quickeneth," or giveth Life. He is spoken of in Romans as "The Spirit of Life." All life is due to the direct action of the Holy Spirit. It is His work to impart to us continually the actual Life of Jesus, who is the true source of Life for both the souls and bodies of God's children . . . It is by the Spirit's fullness and the consequent unhindered quickening that we are "preserved," as Paul says, "spirit, soul and body." Paul says, the Spirit will "quicken ALSO your mortal body," and in 2 Corinthians 4:11 we have the words, "that the Life also of Jesus might be made manifest in our mortal flesh." If you need healing from Christ, wait on God for the Spirit to quicken you to the extent that Mark 11:24 shall be fulfilled in you. This is exactly what the Divine Quickener wants to do for you.[91]

Central to the early Pentecostal doctrine of divine healing is the idea that the life of the risen Christ is imparted by the Spirit as a life-giving

89. Ibid.
90. Bosworth, *Christ the Healer*, 19; emphasis added.
91. Ibid., 151–52, 153.

substance that results in healing. that results in healing. In other words, Jesus is the Healer because he is the essence of life that is imparted by the Holy Spirit.

Jesus Christ the Soon-Coming King

So far we have looked at the first four titles of the Fivefold Gospel in relation to the blessings that were provided in the cross. The activities involved in carrying out the offices of Savior, Sanctifier, Baptizer, and Healer cannot be understood apart from the completion and application of the atoning death of Jesus. So far, what has become evident is that for Pentecostals Christology has been developed in a relational and incarnational mode: who Christ was and is, is always Christ for us and in us. Thus, in relation to the last category of the Fivefold Gospel one might expect that in his role as Soon-Coming King a similar relational perspective might be observed. Such is the case when one considers Jesus as the Coming Bridegroom.

The image of Jesus as the Coming Bridegroom is one that is easily accounted for throughout the writings of early Pentecostalism.[92] In fact a very popular periodical was named *The Bridegroom's Messenger*. In an article in *The Apostolic Faith*, Seymour presented the relationship between Jesus (the Bridegroom) and the church (his Bride) in an allegorical interpretation of Isaac and Rebecca's story in Genesis 24. Interestingly, the role that Eliezer plays in finding a wife for Isaac is the same role that Seymour afforded to the Spirit; it is God's Spirit that selects and prepares the Bride for the Son.[93] W. T. Aiken made a similar allusion in explaining the parable of the ten virgins (Matt 25) when he stated, "the messenger whom God has sent, even the Holy Ghost, to seek and bring the bride for his Son, the heavenly Isaac, is gathering together those who have said [like Rebecca], 'I will go with this man' (Gen 24:58)."[94]

In yet another article, Seymour spoke of the bridal connection between Jesus and his church in more direct association with the work

92. Some articles that present this image include: Aiken, "Bride and the Bridegroom"; Baker, "Bride of Christ," 1, 4; Cotton, "Bride of Christ"; and Seymour, "Rebecca."

93. Seymour, "Rebecca."

94. Aiken, "Bride and the Bridegroom."

of the Spirit: "we are married to Christ now in the Spirit (Rom 7:2, 4)."[95] So significant is the union between the Bridegroom and his Bride in the Spirit that Taylor went so far as to say that the baptism with the Holy Spirit is the seal by which "we are designated as the Bride of the Lamb."[96] Thus, in his ascended state the Christ awaits his Bride who is being adorned with the Spirit until the time of his coming. With this thought one can very well affirm that throughout the history of the Pentecostal movement the relationship between Jesus and the believer is understood in relational terms, from the incarnation until his return. Moreover, it is through the Spirit that the presence of the Risen Christ is made available to believers.

The Challenge of Oneness Christology

Although one could argue that Spirit-Christology provides a better model for constructing a Pentecostal Christology than the traditional Chalcedonian two-natures model, the question of why such an early christological distinctive did not become a central aspect of early Pentecostal Christologies is still left unanswered. For, instead of lengthy explanations that sought to clarify the mystery of Jesus' human and divine natures, there is a stronger emphasis on the significance of the activity of the Spirit in and on the life of Jesus. I suggest that the reason a Spirit-oriented Christology did not surface is twofold. On the one hand, early Pentecostals' theological contribution was obscured by their almost complete dependence on non-Pentecostal theologies in teaching theology and writing doctrinal statements and books. On the other hand, due to the challenge presented by Oneness Pentecostalism many of the christological themes that were articulated formally in a systematic way were of a reactionary nature. Thus, seeking to maintain an evangelically orthodox position and to disassociate themselves from Oneness Pentecostalism, early Pentecostal thinkers developed a Christology more in line with Chalcedon and did not explore their unique Pentecostal emphases.

95. Seymour, "Holy Ghost and the Bride."

96. Taylor, *Spirit and the Bride*; excerpt reprinted in Jacobsen, *Reader in Pentecostal Theology*, 61.

Origins of Oneness Pentecostalism

Oneness Pentecostalism refers to an early branch of Pentecostalism that split in 1916 from the Assemblies of God (AG) over the issue of the Trinity.[97] Significantly, this schism took place only two years after the AG was officially established as a Pentecostal denomination, and it prompted the "Statement of Fundamental Truths" assuring the Trinitarian understanding of the AG. Gary B. McGee comments on the development of the statement in relation to the Oneness movement as follows:

> When the Oneness issue threatened to split the General Council [of the AG] at its gathering in 1916, church leaders willingly set aside the anticreedal sentiments of the Hot Springs meeting by drawing doctrinal boundaries to protect the integrity of the Church and welfare of the saints. Several leading ministers, led by Daniel W. Kerr, drafted the Statement of Fundamental Truths; it contained a long section upholding the orthodox view of the Trinity.[98]

David K. Bernard, a leading Oneness theologian, describes the split this way:

> In 1916 the Assemblies of God adopted a strong, detailed trinitarian statement that caused Oneness preachers to leave the two-year old organization. Some trinitarian preachers left also, because the church had violated its founding principle of adopting no creed other than the Bible. Those that remained in

97. For a brief but authoritative introduction to the origins and theology of the movement, see Reed, "Oneness Pentecostalism."

98. McGee, "Historical Background," 21. Interestingly, in the original "Statement of Fundamental Truths" adopted in October 1916 by the Assemblies of God General Council, their Trinitarian view of God, entitled "The Essential as to the Godhead," appears as the thirteenth statement in a section that is about one-third the length of the seventeen fundamental truths. Moreover, in the "Combined Minutes of the General Council of the Assemblies of God" adopted in 1920, the discussion of the Trinity no longer appears within the "Statement of Fundamental Truths." Instead the now sixteen "Fundamental Truths" are followed by an addendum, also entitled "The Essential as to the Godhead," which further explains the meaning of the second fundamental truth, "The One True God." The reason for this is that the "Fundamental Truths" were the basic biblical teachings upon which the church was founded, and the "Trinity" and "Persons" were terms that did not appear in the biblical text. More recently, however, the addendum has been incorporated to the sixteen "Fundamental Truths" within the second statement, under the heading "The Adorable Godhead."

the Assemblies of God felt that the Oneness believers were in doctrinal error, but at no time did they classify them as a non-Christian cult.[99]

Thus, on both fronts, the reason for the split was differences in belief concerning the doctrine of the Trinity.[100] But the Trinitarian disputes resulted from the distinctive doctrine of the name of Jesus developed by some early Pentecostal leaders (e.g., Frank Ewart, Garfield T. Haywood, and Andrew Urshan). At stake were the establishment of the correct baptismal formula and the prospect of what to do about the re-baptisms that were taking place within the denomination. As a result of Oneness Pentecostals' emphasis on the correct baptismal formula being only "in the name of Jesus" (following Acts 2:38 and 19:5) their opponents called them "Jesus Only." But Oneness Pentecostals have characteristically referred to their understanding of the Godhead as the "New Issue" or "Jesus' Name."[101]

The Origin of the Oneness View of Jesus

Originally, the question was whether it was correct to baptize using the Trinitarian formula ("in the name of the Father, and of the Son, and of the Holy Spirit," Matt 28:19) or to baptize in the name of Jesus only (Acts 2:38; 19:5). The insistence of Oneness preachers on the "Jesus' Name" formula resulted in the adoption of what some describe as a type of theological modalism.[102] An extended quotation from Oneness

99. Bernard, *Oneness View of Jesus*, 142.

100. Although one can find articles and references to the "Trinity" in the early stage of Pentecostalism, it is after the Oneness challenge that a sustained attack is articulated concerning the "New Issue." The immediate effects of the split caused by doctrinal disputes concerning the Trinity can be seen in the edition of *The Weekly Evangel* that was published just after the AG General Council meeting in October 1916. Significantly, an article therein states that the issue of the Trinity was the principal theme of discussion. Frodsham, "Notes from an Eyewitness," 5. Other significant articles that addressed the Trinity and the Oneness view of God include: Hagnes, "Trinity"; Hamilton, "Trinity in the Godhead"; Hughes, "New Light a Fallacy"; Jamieson, "Trinity"; Johnson, "Against False Doctrines"; Lee, "Trinity Finally in One"; idem, "Three in One"; Llewellyn, "Distinction in the Godhead"; Rollins, "Composed of Three"; Thorhill, "Trinity"; Watson, "Great Is the Mystery"; and Williams, "Godhead."

101. Bernard, *Oneness of God*, 15.

102. Anderson, *Introduction to Pentecostalism*, 47. See also McRoberts, "Holy Trinity," 172.

pioneer Andrew D. Urshan will help retrieve the understanding of the theology of "The Name."

> Here is the great Commissioner, The Lord Jesus Christ, sending forth his chosen and appointed commission—commanding them that they should wait until they are fully supplied and empowered from on high (Luke 24:48–49), then go forth to do only one thing, and that specific duty is applied unto His own Person; as He said: "ye shall be witnesses unto me." Thus, we see the definite and positive purpose and service of the Great Christian Commission, viz.: "Go ye therefore and teach all nations, baptizing then IN THE NAME"; notice, please, it is not written in the names, but IN THE NAME. Just as commercial and political commissions are sent forth in the name of the highest office of the government, exactly so the divine commission from the beginning has been sent forth in the one great NAME of the Almighty God. The interesting question is then whose name is this mentioned "NAME" in Matthew 28:19, in which the great Christian commission should go forth . . . It is the one name of the T-H-R-E-E–O-N-E God (1 John 5:7), yea the NAME of the Father, of the Son and of the Holy Ghost.[103]

At the end of the chapter, Urshan stated what he meant more bluntly: "The Name of the Father, of the Son, and of the Holy Ghost, which is the *Lord Jesus Christ.*"[104] Before this culminating statement, though, Urshan included the testimony of a lady who came to understand "the Godhead in Jesus Christ," in order to restate his doctrine of "The Name" in simpler terms.

> [I]n the silence of the night the blessed Spirit spoke to her saying, "Have you a father and a son?" She said, "Yes." Then the Spirit asked her, "Is your father's name Father?" She said, "No, it is Clarence." Then God asked her, "What is the name of your Heavenly Father?" She honestly and prayerfully thought and thought, but she could answer nothing. Then the Spirit proceeded, "What is the name of the Son of the Father?" She said, "Jesus Christ." Then the Spirit proceeded, "Has your Heavenly Father a name; if so, what is it; don't you want to know it?" and He graciously showed her that *Jesus* was the name of our God, our Saviour, and *Christ* was the anointed One which stands for

---

103. Urshan, *Almighty God*, 41–42.

104. Ibid., 50; emphasis added.

the Name and *the fullness of the Holy Ghost in Him*, and the *Lord*
was the name of the Father and all the Deity.[105]

What becomes clear in these two quotations is the equivalency that is
made between the phrases "Father, Son, and Holy Spirit" and "Lord Jesus
Christ."[106] But even more telling is the direct association that Urshan
later made between Jesus and the Spirit under the heading "The Name
of the Holy Ghost in Jesus Christ":

> In the Syriac translation and also in the Greek the Holy Ghost
> is not called "the Comforter," as in the English version (John
> 14:26), but is called "the Parakleta." Jesus Christ bears this very
> same name of the Spirit in 1 John 2:1. (See the Scofield Bible,
> page 1136.) The Holy Ghost is called "the quickening Spirit," so
> is the Lord Jesus called "the quickening Spirit." Compare John
> 6:63 with 1 Cor. 15:45. The Holy Ghost is also called "the Lord."
> Thank God, Jesus Christ is "the Lord" also. The Holy Spirit is
> called "the Spirit of the Lord" and "the Spirit of Christ."[107]

Just as was made evident in the previous discussion of early Pentecostal
Christology, the Spirit in relation to Jesus is crucial for understanding
his person, although Oneness Pentecostals approach it in a wholly different way. Moreover, the prospect of Spirit-Christology serving as a
model for Oneness Pentecostal Christology becomes not only reasonable but viable.

The Promise of Spirit-Christology
for Intra-Pentecostal Dialogue

At this point I would be getting ahead of myself by giving a more ample
explanation of how Oneness Christology can be aptly developed using

---

105. Ibid., 45–46; emphasis added.

106. This was not a new doctrine developed by Andrew Urshan, for it had already
been formulated at the inception of the Oneness movement. The Canadian evangelist
R. E. McAlister had already affirmed at the Arroyo Seco Pentecostal camp meeting of
April 1913 that "the apostles baptized in the name of the Lord Jesus Christ (variations
in Acts) instead of the triune name commanded by Jesus (Matt 28:19)" because "they
understood 'Lord-Jesus-Christ' to be the christological equivalent of 'Father-Son-Holy
Spirit.'" David Reed comments that this short meditation was responsible for the lat-
ter "revelation" of the truth of baptism in the name of the Lord Jesus Christ. Reed,
"Oneness Pentecostalism," 937.

107. Urshan, *Almighty God*, 46.

the model of Spirit-Christology. Yet, given the recent interest with the scholarly discussion of the promise and problem of Spirit-Christology among Pentecostal theologians, it must be stated that even this very divisive issue early in our own tradition can find a better arena for dialogue by adopting this model. For Oneness Pentecostalism was not a late aberration of classical Pentecostalism; it originated during the initial phase of Pentecostalism's worldwide birth and expansion. And yet, we have still to deal with the repercussions of the division caused by the challenge that Oneness Pentecostalism presented in its view of Jesus as God in the flesh.

The key problematic that arose was that for those in the Trinitarian Pentecostal camp, the Oneness view of Jesus was understood as a modern day modalist Christology; for the Oneness perspective Jesus is "God" in the full sense of the meaning, where no other person exists in the Godhead. Without getting into the hundred-year-old argument in defense of either position, let me just say that the main problem of the rupture was the absolute embrace of the Trinitarian concept of God and along with a Logos Christology that made no room for any other understanding of Jesus' divinity that did not promote his pre-existence. In this regard, I believe that Spirit-Christology may serve as a catalyst in repairing the gulf that divides Oneness and Trinitarian Pentecostalism. Could it be that by approaching Christology from a pneumatological orientation, a central aspect of both of these traditions, that we may at least agree that our views are not completely mutually exclusive? Though I realize that the differences in thought are not easily resolved, in many ways I do believe they are not absolutely insurmountable. It is my hope that the turn to Spirit-Christology will provide fertile ground for theological discussion and that in the years to come this model will serve to unite us in our continued experience of Jesus through the Spirit. At the end of the next chapter I will return to this issue and propose some avenues of reflection that might assists Pentecostals (Oneness and Trinitarians) in their quest to understand together the meaning of the full deity of Jesus from a pneumatological perspective.

2

The Recent Charismatic/Pentecostal Turn toward Spirit-Christology

SINCE SOME EARLY PENTECOSTAL WRITERS REFLECTED UPON THE person and work of Jesus using a pneumatological framework, we can say that Spirit-Christology is a characteristically Pentecostal model for doing Christology. This chapter outlines how Spirit-Christology can be a helpful paradigm for recovering the Pentecostal christological heritage and for developing a Christology that truly reflects the Pentecostal theological imagination.

The plan for this chapter is as follows. First, I will show that Pentecostal Christology needs to move beyond Chalcedonian Christology—without abandoning it totally—in order to make a distinctive contribution. Second, I will trace the biblical origins and early development of Spirit-Christology as a backdrop for understanding the promise and problems inherent within the model. Third, I will explore various recent non-Pentecostal proposals for Spirit-Christology, shedding light on potential difficulties that cannot be avoided in plotting a course for Christology using this paradigm. Fourth, I will examine the contributions of some innovative Pentecostal proposals to a pneumatologically oriented model for Christology, and propose some guidelines for a Pentecostal Spirit-Christology. Fifth, I will make an overall analysis of the potential of Spirit-Christology by outlining how the model is helpful for navigating the most crucial christological challenge that confronts Pentecostal theology from within: the Oneness view of Jesus.

Moving Beyond a Chalcedonian Christology

Judging from the pneumatological orientation of Pentecostal thought, one might suspect that Spirit-Christology would provide a congenial model for developing a Pentecostal Christology. However, Pentecostal approaches to systematic theology reveal a preference for a Chalcedonian two-natures understanding of the person and work of Jesus Christ.[1] For the most part, Pentecostals have traditionally borrowed their theological frameworks from other evangelical traditions and baptized them as their own.[2]

One might say that most of the early Pentecostal works, and even some more recent ones, were rehashed works with added appendices on the key doctrines emphasized by Pentecostals, of which the baptism with the Holy Spirit is primary. For example, Myer Pearlman's *Knowing*

---

1. By a "Chalcedonian two-natures paradigm" I mean the model developed in the Council of Chalcedon in 451 CE, which defined the doctrine of the two natures (the divine and the human) in the person of Jesus Christ. The full text of the Chalcedonian definition reads:

> Following, therefore, the holy fathers, we confess one and the same Son, who is our Lord Jesus Christ, and we all agree in teaching that this very same Son is complete in his deity and complete—the very same—in his humanity, truly God and truly a human being, this very same one being composed of a rational soul and a body, coessential with the Father as to his deity and coessential with us—the very same one—as to his humanity, being like us in every aspect apart from sin . . . acknowledged to be unconfusedly, unalterably, undividedly, inseparably in two natures, since the difference of the natures is not destroyed because of the union, but on the contrary, the character of each nature is preserved and comes together in one person and one hypostasis, not divided or torn into two persons but one and the same Son. Norris, *Christological Controversy*, 159.

Significantly, this translation is quoted and wholeheartedly defended in Stanley Horton's Pentecostal systematic theology. Moreover, when examining various Pentecostal works in systematic theology this provides the basic framework for explaining the divinity and humanity of Jesus Christ. Nichols, "Lord Jesus Christ," 319.

2. Commenting on the prospect of a distinctively Pentecostal theology, Clark Pinnock (a Baptist non-Pentecostal who is highly sympathetic to this movement) considered that the major problem obstructing the development of a Pentecostal systematic theology is the continued dependence on textbooks written by fundamentalists and post-fundamentalists. He correctly points out that in many Pentecostal institutions textbooks like Millard Erickson's or Norman L. Geisler's systematic theologies, among others, have become the standard textbooks, although they are neither Pentecostal nor do they advance a pneumatology that is in line with Pentecostal thought. Pinnock, "Divine Relationality," 24. Even more illuminating is the admission by a leading Pentecostal theologian, Cheryl Bridges Johns, that "there is inherent within the ranks of Pentecostal believers an inferiority complex which assumes that non-Pentecostals know more than we do and do things better than we can." Johns, *Pentecostal Formation*, 7.

the Doctrines of the Bible[3] could be read almost in its entirety without the reader being aware that the author is a prominent Pentecostal theologian and scholar,[4] for throughout his discussion of the person and work of Jesus Christ, Pearlman merely reiterates what traditional evangelical systematic theologies affirm about Jesus' divinity and humanity without the least bit of Pentecostal flavor.[5]

More recently, the Pentecostal *Systematic Theology* edited by Stanley M. Horton (Assemblies of God minister and scholar) develops its christological themes along similar lines, though in some respects it is overall more characteristically Pentecostal. The outline followed in chapter 9, "The Lord Jesus Christ," which develops the book's Christology, is as follows:

1. Knowledge of Jesus

2. Issues in Methodology

3. A New Testament Understanding of Jesus

4. Heresies Concerning the Natures of Jesus Christ

5. Systematic Considerations in Christology

Significantly, only in the last section of the chapter is something said that is distinctively Pentecostal. After a discussion of the virgin birth and an extensive biblical and Chalcedonian overview of the hypostatic union of the divine and human natures in Jesus, there is a short reflection on Jesus and the Holy Spirit.[6] Why not start with Jesus' relationship with

3. Speaking of the influence of this work, Russell P. Spittler comments: "The exemplar of Pentecostal systematic theologies was authored by Myer Pearlman. . . . In use continuously for nearly a half century, *Knowing the Doctrines of the Bible* is subtly competent in its conception though simple in language. It has been translated into Spanish and several other languages, and the volume finds wide use by Pentecostal missionaries in the task of training national ministers for evangelism. Within the Pentecostal movement no volume has rivaled the influence of Myer Pearlman's doctrinal handbook." Spittler, "Scripture and the Theological Enterprise," 65.

4. Douglas Jacobsen describes Pearlman's theology as "traditional and orthodox in content." In a sense, his attempt is to link Pentecostal beliefs to traditional Christian doctrines that are understood as defining orthodox Christianity. However, it seems that in his attempt to show the continuity of Pentecostal beliefs to orthodox doctrines, "the experiential dimension of the first-generation Pentecostal faith" is nowhere to be found. Jacobsen, "Knowing the Doctrines of Pentecostals," 94.

5. Pearlman, *Knowing the Doctrines*.

6. To be fair, in some respects these short reflections constitute an incipient Spirit-Christology, for many other non-Pentecostal authors of their time would have skipped

the Spirit? Why not make this a central aspect of the book's portrayal of Pentecostal Christology instead of relegating it to what amounts to an aside at the end of the chapter? Why not opt for a pneumatologically oriented Christology, one that emphasizes the role of the Spirit in the earthly life and ministry of Jesus and his continued presence and work in and through the Spirit?

Although all theologies unavoidably build on the theological traditions that precede them, they need not accept them blindly. One cannot, as it were, develop a Christology in a theological vacuum. Yet, the constructive task of theology requires that it be critical of its foundations and its methods if it is not to merely repeat past thought patterns and pretend to be relevant for today. Thus, it becomes imperative that one not be so enamored with theological constructs that no longer speak in a relevant way to our contemporary situation that one cannot look fairly and critically at other models.

As useful as the Chalcedonian two-natures model has been, there is room for other models that serve a complementary role, for no one model can exhaust the christological themes found in the biblical narrative.[7] Tatha Wiley expresses the need for new ways of understanding Jesus' significance in light of modernity:

> While these ways of understanding [the person and work of Jesus Christ], found in the New Testament, the great creeds, and theological tradition, are rich and deep, they do not necessarily function effectively today in communicating the meaning they once did. For contemporary faith to remain vibrant, we must articulate the significance of Jesus for ourselves. We need to draw

---

any mention of the relationship of Jesus and the Holy Spirit. In retrospect, one might say that they lacked the tools and models to speak of Spirit-Christology in the ways this has more recently been articulated. What is more, this brief pneumatologically oriented reflection on Jesus was also an important theme in earlier Pentecostal systematic theologies. See Nichols, "Lord Jesus Christ," 323–24; and especially, Williams, *Systematic Theology*, 3:16–17 (the section entitled "His [the Holy Spirit's] Work in Our Lord Jesus").

7. Helpful in this respect is William P. Loewe's analysis of classical Christology and its shortcomings in addressing contemporary issues. For example, he notes that due to the modern psychological conception of person that stresses a cognitive personhood, "it has become unintelligible to speak of Christ as someone who is fully human but not a human person." Loewe, "Classical Christology," 62.

> on terms and categories both meaningful to us and appropriate
> for our time.[8]

From a Pentecostal perspective, then, what are the key questions guiding christological talk? Is the governing idea the need to provide an ontological framework that explains the internal relationship between the divine and human natures in the person of Jesus? Or does the Pentecostal tradition lend itself more toward a functional Christology that seeks to define who Jesus is for today by what he did during his earthly ministry?

It is my perception that limiting Pentecostal Christology to a Chalcedonian framework will inevitably bifurcate its potential by ignoring one of Pentecostalism's most important contributions: the centrality of the experience of the Spirit. Ralph Del Colle highlights the significance of the Pentecostal experience on christological thought in the following way:

> What is peculiar to the Pentecostal experience is that this basic truth [that God's presence is mediated by the Risen Lord in the Holy Spirit], which characterizes all genuine Christian initiation, is marked by an experimental effusion of the Spirit as gift and empowerment.[9]

Indeed, Pentecostals' christological imagination is intrinsically wedded to their pneumatological orientation, for they experience Jesus' presence through the Spirit and understand every manifestation of the Spirit today as, metaphorically speaking, a breath of Jesus (John 20:22).

It therefore becomes increasingly important for Pentecostals to develop their theology in their own distinctive way. In the areas of pneumatology and ecclesiology, various works of theology from a strictly Pentecostal perspective have appeared, yet this is not true of Christology. While exploring christological models that may give more prominence to the presence and activity of the Spirit is one possibility, perhaps a better model for such an undertaking is found in Spirit-Christology; by adopting it Pentecostals will be helped to develop a Christology that is shaped with pneumatological contours. But this in itself is not a novel idea: some notable Pentecostal scholars have long

---

8. Wiley, "Thinking of Christ," 15.
9. Del Colle, "Spirit-Christology," 93.

since made the turn toward Spirit-Christology.[10] And though one might advocate for its rigorous application to any Pentecostal Christology, one does well to ask, what have been the limitations of this model in previous approaches to Spirit-Christology? We saw in the previous chapter that underdeveloped themes in early Pentecostal Christology indicate that indeed Spirit-Christology offers a distinctively Pentecostal understanding of Jesus. Yet some Pentecostal scholars caution that this model might downplay the divinity of Jesus.

Harold Hunter, for example, offers three cautions.[11] First, in seeking to preserve the humanity of Jesus, Spirit-Christology robs him of his full divinity by making the Spirit the presence or inspiration of God on his life. Second, the model does not conform to the orthodox teaching of Chalcedon about Jesus as truly God and truly man. Third, it reduces the Spirit from being a person to being a divine influence. Significantly, his discussion of Spirit-Christology is located in an excursus within a chapter on the doctrine of salvation. This is important because ultimately Hunter rejects Spirit-Christology on soteriological grounds. In other words, as much as Pentecostals might want to explore Spirit-Christology because of its seemingly natural fit with Pentecostal distinctives, one should be cautious of uncritically accepting a model that portrays a Jesus who is unable to save humanity of his own accord due to his being also merely human.

To respond to these allegations now would be getting ahead of myself. But it helps to have them in mind as we present past and recent proposals for Spirit-Christology. In this vein, I turn now to the biblical origins and early development of Spirit-Christology in order to establish the key issues that, from its inception, needed to be reckoned with, mainly in terms of an adoptionist Christology.

Spirit-Christology: Biblical Origins and Early Development

Spirit-Christology is not a novel concept that has no historical warrant. In fact, it is considered at all only because it already was a viable model not only for the church fathers but even for the New Testament authors.

10. Later in this chapter, I will discuss Amos Yong's and S. D. L. Jenkins' proposals for a Pentecostal Spirit-Christology.

11. Hunter, *Spirit-Baptism*, 212–30.

What, then, are its original contours, and how do these illuminate its current trajectories?

Piet Schoonenberg argues that there is not one unifying Christology in the Gospels but rather various complementary Christologies.[12] Both Mark and Luke, for example, contain Spirit-Christologies, but also Son of Man Christologies. Paul W. Newman comments, "there is an immense amount of evidence in the New Testament directly linking Jesus and God's Spirit."[13] Whether one begins with the Gospels or with Paul, the biblical testimony undoubtedly contains glimpses of a Spirit-Christology in the making.

Beginning with the Gospels and specifically with the birth narratives of Matthew and Luke, there is no question that the evangelists ascribe to the Spirit a definitive role in the personhood of the incarnate Son of God. In Luke, the birth of Jesus is described as having taken place under the providential care of the Spirit.[14] The imagery used is that of the Spirit coming upon (ἐπελεύσεται) Mary and the power of the Most High hovering over or overshadowing (ἐπισκιάσει) her (Luke 1:35). As a result of the Spirit's presence on and over Mary, the infant born will be "holy" and called "Son of God".[15] The Spirit's activity at the time of Jesus' conception highlights the inseparability of the two throughout the earthly life of Jesus and, Schoonenberg suggests, even from his conception.[16]

Matthew makes explicit what Luke mentions only implicitly: twice he speaks of Jesus' conception as a work of the Spirit. First, he states that Mary "was found to be with child from [ἐκ] the Holy Spirit" (Matt 1:18). Then, after Joseph had secretly decided to leave Mary, the angel spoke to him saying, "do not be afraid to take Mary as your wife, for the child

---

12. Schoonenberg, *El Espíritu, la Palabra y el Hijo*, 48.

13. Newman, *Spirit Christology*, 27.

14. Meier, *Marginal Jew*, 220–22.

15. Piet Schoonenberg argues that Luke is not explicit in saying that from the moment of conception Jesus is called the "Son of God" because his divine sonship is spoken of in the future tense (κληθήσεται). However, the future tense is used here to speak of a future event, and not necessarily as a theological commentary on Jesus' becoming "Son of God" at a later time (i.e., Jesus' is not yet "Son of God" at conception but until his baptism). In other words, as Luke states that the "Spirit will come upon [Mary]" (future tense) and in that future time the child "will be called Son of God" (Luke 1:35). Schoonenberg, *El Espíritu, la Palabra y el Hijo*, 26.

16. Ibid., 25–26.

conceived [γεννηθὲν] in her is from [ἐκ] the Holy Spirit" (Matt 1:20).[17] There is no question then that the Spirit's work made the conception of Jesus possible and that for this reason the Son's and the Spirit's missions became interdependent and interpenetrating.

The next major occurrence that the evangelists record about the life of Jesus is his baptism at the Jordan. Here too the Spirit has a prominent role. All three Synoptic Gospels mention in their own unique way that the Holy Spirit descended upon Jesus after he came out of the baptismal waters (Mark 1:10; Matt 3:16; Luke 3:22), and that the Spirit sent him forth into the desert to be tempted immediately after his baptism (Mark 1:12; Matt 4:1; Luke 4:1).[18] Luke even goes so far as to equate the descent of the Spirit on Jesus as an act of being filled with the Spirit, for later he comments that "full of the Holy Spirit" Jesus was led to the desert (Luke 4:1).

Continuing with this theme of Jesus' fullness with the Spirit, Luke posits that his whole ministry was carried out in the power and anointing of the Spirit. In a synagogue of his hometown of Nazareth, he read from the text of the prophet Isaiah (61:1): "The Spirit of the Lord is on me, because he has anointed me to preach good news to the poor" (Luke 4:18). Later, in Acts, Luke preserves a sermon of Peter's, which expands on the activity of the Spirit in Jesus' earthly ministry. Peter says, "... God anointed Jesus of Nazareth with the Holy Spirit and power, and ... he went around doing good and healing all who were under the power of the devil, because God was with him" (Acts 10:38). Here again an intrinsic connection is made between Jesus' mission and the role of the Spirit in his life.

Spirit-Christology in the biblical record is not limited to the life and earthly ministry of Jesus, but encompasses his ongoing presence

17. Following Meier's analysis, Colin Brown comments that just as with Mary (1:16) and the other four women mentioned in Matthew's genealogy—Tamar (1:3), Rahab and Ruth (1:5), Uriah's wife (1:6)—the Holy Spirit's role in the conception of Jesus is likened as to the females and not the typical male used to describe it. "The use of evk followed by a woman's name follows a pattern, which suggests that the phrase ἐκ πνεύματός (1:18) indicates that the Spirit plays a female role in the conception of Jesus." Brown, "Role of the Spirit," 2.

18. Significantly, at this juncture, after his baptism and before the temptations, Luke states that Jesus began his public ministry (Luke 3:23). The inclusion of this statement seems to imply that Jesus was made ready for his public ministry only after the Holy Spirit came upon him.

as the glorified Christ. For example, in the Book of Acts, Peter attributes the pouring out of the Spirit to Jesus: "Exalted to the right hand of God, he has received from the Father the promised Holy Spirit and has poured out what you now see and hear" (2:33). In addition, the apostle Paul enigmatically states that the Spirit of holiness confirmed Jesus' divine sonship either by or from the resurrection (Rom 1:4).

What then does Jesus' divinity have to do with the Spirit? Does Jesus' divinity stem from the Spirit's activity at his conception? If so, does the Spirit communicate the divine attributes to the humanity of Jesus or is the Spirit merely the agent of the divine Son's transmutation into the human Son of God? If instead Jesus' divinity begins at the time of his baptism, does the Holy Spirit's descent on the Son signal the beginning of his adoption as the Son of God? Or is Jesus' resurrection from the dead not only God's stamp of approval on his life but also his entry into the divine life? It is these questions that modern pneumatologically-oriented theologians seek to answer. Yet, before we turn to these we must first take a look at the earliest theological constructions of Spirit-Christology found in the church fathers, for they serve to outline the various ways in which the relation of Jesus and the Spirit have been understood.

Perhaps one of the earliest Spirit-Christologies to be penned was that contained in *The Shepherd* by Hermas, a Jewish Christian living around the middle of the second century AD. *The Shepherd* is written in apocalyptic style and imagery. In this book, an angel gives his message through five visions, and imparts commandments and ten similitudes. In the fifth similitude, which relates to fasting, the Shepherd tells a parable, which has many similarities to the parable of the laborers (Matt 20:1–16). In the Shepherd's parable, however, Jesus is a servant who works the field and is beloved by the owner of the vineyard. Moreover, the owner himself has a beloved son, but because of the beloved servant's hard labor he is made co-heir with the son. Not content with the Shepherd's first explanation of the parable, the author asks to know the deeper meaning of the parable. And after some deliberation the Shepherd replies, "The field is this world, and the lord of the field is the one who created all things and completed them and empowered them. The son is the Holy Spirit and the slave is the Son of God."[19] As odd as

19. Significantly, the earlier translation of the *Shepherd of Hermas* (1919) in the Loeb Classical Library omits the phrase "The son is the Holy Spirit," yet notes that "with

this expression might seem from a post-Chalcedonian perspective, the rest of the passage indicates that in fact the *Shepherd of Hermas* here embarks on an early understanding of Spirit-Christology.

Astonishingly, the text of *The Shepherd* does not include either "Jesus" or "Christ." When speaking of Jesus the term used is always Son of God (υἱὸς θεου). But who is this Son of God according to Hermas? A little further in the passage, Hermas further explains his understanding of the Son of God:

> God made the Holy Spirit dwell in the flesh that he [Or: it] desired, even though it preexisted and created all things. This flesh, then, in which the Holy Spirit dwelled, served well as the Spirit's slave, for it conducted itself in reverence and purity, not defiling the Spirit at all. Since it lived in a pure and good way, cooperating with the Spirit and working with it in everything it did, behaving in a strong and manly way, *God chose it to be a partner with the Holy Spirit.* For the conduct of this flesh was pleasing, because it was not defiled on earth while bearing the Holy Spirit. *Thus he took his Son and the glorious angels as counselors,* so that this flesh, which served blamelessly as the Spirit's slave, might have a place of residence and not appear to have lost the reward for serving as a slave. For all flesh in which the Spirit has dwelled—and which has been found undefiled and spotless—will receive a reward.[20]

The basic principle expounded here is the idea that the Holy Spirit is the preexistent person of the Son of God.[21] In other words, the Holy Spirit, which here equates to divinity, became incarnate in the flesh (i.e., Jesus' humanity) of the Son of God. In the parable, the son of the master is the Spirit and the slave is the Son of God. According to his own interpretation, Hermas understood the blameless life of the servant and fleshly

---

the text given it must be noted that the Son [referring to the master's son] in the parable remains unexplained." *Shepherd of Hermas, Sim.* 5.5.2 (1919). In the newer translation (2003), the phrase ὁ δὲ υἱὸς τὸ πνευμα τὸ ἅγιόν ἐστιν appears with an indication that an early second-century Latin manuscript includes it, although it is omitted by later manuscripts. It is probable that scribes copying the original text after the fourth or fifth centuries would have stumbled over this phrase because of the apparent heretical identification of the Son with the Spirit. *Shepherd of Hermas* 59.2 (2003). The phrase "the son is the Holy Spirit" is more likely to have been part of the original reading because it is the more difficult reading.

20. *Shepherd of Hermas* 59.5–7 (2003); emphasis added.

21. Schoonenberg, *El Espíritu, la Palabra y el Hijo,* 83.

Son of God as meritorious of assumption into the divine life. Having been an undefiled Spirit-bearer, the flesh of the Son of God, Jesus' humanity, received its reward: participation in the divine nature.

What becomes clear, then, is that Hermas' christological interests are moral. The Spirit-Christology he develops functions as a moral recommendation, for the Son of God serves as a model in the service of God. Daniel Ruiz Bueno explains it as follows:

> The Son of God is our model in the work of fervor and generosity in service of the divine; for, having been made human, he worked harder than he should have—truly, he did not need to—for our salvation. He made himself a slave in the labor of the vineyard that his Father put him in charge of. His flesh, his humanity, faithful and loyal servant to the Spirit, that is to say, to his divinity. This moral and exemplary aspect of the work of the Son of God Hermas sees clearly, and it is what he intends to propose to his readers.[22]

What is significant to note in Hermas' parabolic Spirit-Christology is that he is not interested in explaining the relation between the pre-existent Spirit and the Father, and he also does not explain the constitution of the Spirit's union with Jesus' humanity. His is an incipient Spirit-Christology that provides fertile terrain for theological speculation.

Indeed, if one were to make a close inspection of the incipient Spirit-Christologies of other early church fathers, similar fragmentary christological statements would be found in which the relation of the Spirit to Jesus is simply alluded to but not clearly defined. Clement of Rome, for example, seems to border on a Spirit-Christology when he states, "Jesus Christ—the Lord who saved us—was first spirit (πνευμα) and then became flesh . . ." (2 Clem. 5:9).[23] Moreover, seeking to explain the twofold nativity of Jesus, Lactantius writes, "For he was twice born: first of God, in the spirit, before the origin of the world; afterwards, in the flesh of man, in the reign of Augustus" (Epitome 43). These pneumatic expressions of Christology, however, would shortly be replaced

---

22. Bueno, Padres Apostólicos, 925; my translation.

23. Interestingly, in a significantly late manuscript (c. 1056) πνευμα is replaced by λόγος. This apparently innocent gloss could very well point to the tendency of replacing an earlier Spirit-Christology with the Logos Christology of the later church fathers and councils.

by Logos-type Christologies, which evidently were born in connection to Spirit-Christology.

According to Schoonenberg's analysis, Spirit-Christology began to wane in relevance and popularity because of its natural connection to Christologies of the Word (λόγος).[24] Because πνευμα already functioned as a symbol for the divine and the concept of λογός connected ideally with Hellenistic culture, it would not be long before the two would be used synonymously in christological discussions. A primary example of this tendency is found in Justin Martyr, who wrote, "It is wrong, therefore, to understand the Spirit and the Power of God as anything else than the Word, who is also the first-born of God" (*Apology* 1.33). Thus, in an effort to recover Spirit-Christology as a Christology in its own right, various treatments of Spirit-Christology have appeared recently, some promising, and some prompting labels of heresy.

Recent Non-Pentecostal and Charismatic Proposals for Spirit-Christology

The promise and problems of recent proposals in Spirit-Christology can be summarized within three categories: replacement, revisionist, and complementary.[25] Theologians who opt for the first model in their construction of Spirit-Christology seek to replace the traditional two-natures Chalcedonian Christology with one that pretends to be more relevant to the questions of the modern mind. By a revisionist Spirit-Christology what is meant is a proposal that aims to revise dogmatic

---

24. Schoonenberg, *El Espíritu, la Palabra y el Hijo*, 84–85.

25. After reviewing various typologies for recent attempts at Spirit-Christology, I decided that these three categories are more suitable to explain the differences in competing proposals. Ralph Del Colle divides the Spirit-Christology camp into two: on the one hand, those that propose a revisionary post-Chalcedonian alternative to classical Christologies (including Geoffrey Lampe, Paul Newman, and Roger Haight among others); and on the other hand, those that propose an orthodox Spirit-Christology (including his own Trinitarian proposal and those of others such as Jürgen Moltmann). Del Colle, "Spirit-Christology," 97–98. Another similar typology is that of Myk Habets, who simply differentiates between "those that seek to complement Logos Christology with a Spirit-Christology, and those that seek to replace Logos Christology with a Spirit-Christology." Habets, "Spirit Christology," 203. I think this sort of either/or designation is somewhat simplistic and does not leave room for anything in between. As can be gleaned from my designations, I simply rearrange the three already offered options by placing a revisionist model in between the replacement and complementary ones.

christological statements in such a way as to reinterpret them with new understandings and definitions, but not completing throwing them out. The third category is one that lays out a more complementary way in which a Chalcedonian or Logos Christology may be expounded alongside a Spirit-Christology in such a manner that it gives equal justice to both models.

In the following section I do not pretend to give a full treatment of every mentioned author's Spirit-Christology. Instead I highlight each author's particular perspective as a way of plotting the promise and potential pitfalls of Spirit-Christology as a model in general. In surveying the various Charismatic and Pentecostal Spirit-Christologies, I will show how their proposals differentiate themselves from the non-Pentecostal approaches mentioned.

Replacement Models of Spirit-Christology: Lampe, Newman, and Dunn

Three recent proposals that clearly seek to undermine the continued development of a Logos Christology are those of Geoffrey Lampe, Paul Newman, and James D. G. Dunn. What characterizes all three authors' Spirit-Christology is their rejection of the incarnation and their identification of the Spirit as the divine influence and/or inspiration on or over the man Jesus. Ultimately, in their regard, it is the Spirit who accounts for the divine element in the life of Jesus.

Lampe, for instance, in his *God as Spirit*, does not shy away from expounding an "inspirational" Christology as opposed to an incarnational one. Seeking to understand the two-pronged relation, first, between Jesus and God, and second, between Jesus and believers, Lampe turns to the Spirit who is "God himself as active towards and in his human creation."[26] Accordingly, Lampe understands that God as Spirit

> . . . indwelt and motivated the human spirit of Jesus in such a way that in him, uniquely, the relationship for which man is intended by his Creator was fully realized; that through Jesus God acted decisively to cause men to share in his relationship to God.[27]

26. Lampe, *God as Spirit*, 11.
27. Ibid.

From this perspective, then, he insists that the continued significance of Jesus for Christian believers today should not be his descent as the pre-existent redeemer nor his present existence as the Son of God who sits at the right hand of the Father.[28] In fact, Lampe boldly states that we have no need for a mediator nor a subjective experience of the post-existent Christ, for "[i]t is God himself, disclosed to us and experienced by us as inspiring and indwelling Spirit (or Wisdom or Word), who meets us through Jesus and can make us Christlike."[29] Moreover, with regard to the resurrection, Lampe affirms that there is no need to dispute over the empty tomb, for the fundamental religious question is only answered when we "encounter today the active presence of God the Spirit who was in Jesus and who now renews and recreates us after his likeness."[30] Lampe's proposal culminates in a complete departure from Chalcedonian Christology, so much that he even dispenses with the Trinitarian view of God.

Ralph Del Colle suggests there are three highly controversial shifts that Lampe's Spirit-Christology promotes: (1) "dispens[ing] with the hypostatic distinctions within the triunity of God," (2) a view of the Spirit that is not "as a third hypostatic identity in the Godhead," and (3) "a thorough demythologization of all the christological loci."[31] In opposition to Del Colle, Lampe staunchly insists:

> I believe in the Divinity of our Lord and Saviour Jesus Christ, in the sense that the same one God, the Creator and Saviour Spirit, revealed himself and acted decisively for us in Jesus. I believe in the Divinity of the Holy Ghost, in the sense that the same one God, the Creator and Saviour Spirit, is here and now not very far from every one of us; for in him we live and move, in him we have our being, in us, if we consent to know and trust him, he will create the Christlike harvest: love, joy, peace, patience, kindness, goodness, fidelity, gentleness, and self-control.[32]

It is interesting that Lampe uses the noun "Divinity" to speak of both Jesus and the Spirit and yet in the same breath qualifies it in a way that is clearly non-Trinitarian. What can also be detected from this quota-

28. Ibid., 33.
29. Ibid., 144.
30. Ibid., 152.
31. Del Colle, *Christ and the Spirit*, 163.
32. Lampe, *God as Spirit*, 228.

tion is Lampe's soteriological understanding of Christ's work from the perspective of the moral influence theory. Important to Lampe, then, is not Christ's pre-existence, nor the incarnation or just about any other traditional christological loci, but rather how Jesus' life serves as a model for achieving an existential connection with God and Christlikeness through the same Spirit that was operative in his life—in essence a Spirit-Christology of moral influence.

Very much in line with Lampe's proposal is Paul Newman, who follows him closely, even adopting similar categorical constructions (i.e., his interpersonal and intrapersonal models of Spirit-Christology).[33] In particular, Newman's proposal suggests a Spirit-Christology that "stresses the relational unity of Christ to God without any ontological corollary."[34] In short, he is quite comfortable in promoting an adoptionist position, finding adoption "a useful and appropriate term to describe the covenantal relationship of the children of God, including *Jesus to God*."[35] The main reason for Newman's position is his assumption (shared with Lampe, and as we shall see also with Dunn) about Jesus' inability to be both human and divine. Newman summarizes it like this: "If Jesus was human he could not at the same time be deity. His relationship with God had to be adoptive."[36]

Newman considers that there are two avenues for developing a Spirit-Christology, which can be distinguished from each other according to how the relationship between Jesus and God (as Spirit) is understood; either as interpersonal or intrapersonal. Newman lays out the two as follows:

> An intrapersonal relationship between Jesus and God would presuppose that Jesus' identity as a person was the very identity of God. If Jesus somehow shared the identity of God's personality he could be said to have an intrapersonal relationship with God, assuming that God has only one personality, one centre of consciousness. The relationship between Jesus and God would be like a person talking to herself or himself rather than two persons talking to each other.

33. Newman, *Spirit Christology*, 173.
34. Habets, "Spirit Christology," 208.
35. Newman, *Spirit Christology*, 215; emphasis added.
36. Ibid., 217.

> An interpersonal relationship between Jesus and God the
> Spirit would presuppose that Jesus was a human being with his
> own personality, his own centre of consciousness, his own iden-
> tity which, however Godlike, was nonetheless not the identity or
> centre of consciousness of God's very Self.[37]

Alerting the reader that the "classical christocentric-trinitarian paradigm of Christianity" is highly problematic because it ascribes to the
intrapersonal model,[38] he opts for the interpersonal model as his starting point.

According to Newman, this "[i]nterpersonal Spirit christology
clearly affirms the specific human individuality of Jesus and also affirms that he was full of the Holy Spirit."[39] In fact, the full humanity of
Jesus is not in any way compromised by his being full of the Spirit, but
on the contrary it allowed him to realize "human freedom to such an
extent that he could be called 'the image of the invisible God' (Col 1:15)
or 'the Last Adam' (1 Cor 15:45)."[40] As a result, Newman proposes that
Jesus was just like any other human being, limited yet with the capacity
to grow in knowledge, and in need of forgiveness.[41] That Newman has
gone to the extreme of questioning Jesus' impeccability in order to establish his humanity is very suggestive of what his interpersonal model
says about Jesus' divinity.

Newman does not beat around the bush in order to establish his
opinion concerning Jesus' divinity. He flat out states that

> the presence of the Spirit in Jesus did not make Jesus in himself
> divine, any more than it makes anyone else divine when God is
> present as Spirit. To speak of any human as a divine person is

---

37. Ibid., 172.

38. Newman argues that despite the distinctions within the Godhead (i.e., God as
"three persons") Western Christianity emphasizes in the doctrine of the Trinity, they
still ascribe to the intrapersonal model he develops. The reasoning that accompanies
this judgment is that "[i]t is traditionally recognized in Western Christianity that the
'persons' of the Trinity are not supposed to be conceived as three 'centres of conscious-
ness.'" Ibid.

39. Ibid., 175.

40. Ibid., 177.

41. Newman offers an extended explanation concerning the unwarranted affirmation of Jesus' sinlessness. He argues that "[i]f atonement is conceived in processive
rather than transactional terms, there is no logical necessity to affirm Jesus' sinlessness."
Ibid., 177–78.

to lose the distinction between Creator and creature. This either endangers monotheism with polytheism or amounts to idolatry which is, by definition, to treat a creature as if it were the Creator. To say that Jesus was not a creature is to forfeit any realistic affirmation of his humanness.[42]

However, Newman considers it equally dangerous to propose a functional Christology that infers Jesus' deity on account of God's presence in him, because the logic of this premise is highly problematic if extended to the rest of creation. "Either we must say that God's functioning in Spirit makes the whole universe in which God functions divine and that God's grace in all human morality makes everyone metaphysically divine or else desist from making the claim in connection with Jesus."[43]

In effect, what Newman does by negating completely the divinity of Jesus is establish his full humanity, yet with some difference to ours—the difference being in reference to God's presence. So how does Newman understand the logic of salvation?

> The uniqueness of Jesus' contribution to the salvation of the world lies in his pioneering of faith as well as perfecting of it. His *modus operandi* or *modus vivendi* of salvation is what distinguishes Jesus as Savior more than anything else. Jesus' theology of salvation as the Reigning of God is, of course, very important and especially so in Spirit christology because the Reigning of God and the presence of God as Spirit are identical in substance.
>
> What was truly original and unique was the way in which Jesus *lived* the Reigning of God, embodying it in his own person and actualizing it in his own vocation. Jesus preached and manifested the way of life of the Kingdom of God and called people to follow him in that way of life. He formed and taught a group of disciples to live and preach the Reigning of God as he was doing.
>
> It was Jesus' orthopraxy that constitutes his primary significance for salvation. His way of the cross which was the way of the Spirit and the way of God's Reigning became the definitive meaning on which the church was originally founded.[44]

42. Ibid., 179.

43. Ibid., 181.

44. Ibid., 147–48.

For Newman, salvation is attained when one converts to God's way of life by adopting the values of his Reign.[45] Understood in this sense, Newman rejects any understanding of salvation that presupposes "a once-and-for-all transaction done by Jesus at Calvary."[46] Instead, "Salvation here is understood to be a process of overcoming evil with good . . . a matter of realizing or actualizing of the Reigning of God in Jesus."[47] Accordingly, Jesus is not seen as one who accomplished salvation for all on the cross, but rather as the example of self-sacrifice and love on the way to the cross.

Now, turning back to Jesus' humanity, Newman states that "Jesus is different from other human beings in degree rather than in kind"[48]— meaning that God's presence in Jesus is the same in kind but different in degree "from the way God is present whenever God graces human lives and historical situations."[49] In other words, all humans can have the same sort of inner presence of God as Spirit that inspires them to a life committed to the Reigning of God. The difference is that, unlike all human beings who have the capacity to "incarnate" the presence of God as Spirit, "Jesus is the model for God's incarnation in all people."[50]

What does Newman mean by "incarnation"? First of all, he rejects the understanding of the exclusive incarnation of God in Jesus that equivocally leads to his deification. Instead he opts for an understanding of incarnation that is synonymous with inspiration, explaining his position in this way:

> On the symbolic basis of wind or breath, God as Spirit can be said to *inspire* people. On the symbolic basis of fire God as Spirit can be said to ignite, inflame or enlighten people with Godly power and meaning. On the symbolic basis of water God can be said to infuse or "pour into" people all the goodness of grace, and on the symbolic basis of earth or matter, God can be said to upbuild people into a spiritual dwelling place. None of these metaphorical ways of describing God's presence in human life suggest any displacement of humanness or reduction in human

45. Ibid., 148.
46. Ibid., 164.
47. Ibid.
48. Ibid., 182.
49. Ibid.
50. Ibid., 184.

identity by reason of God's presence. If incarnation is used in conjunction with these metaphors it can be a legitimate and valuable term, but if incarnation is used *in contrast to* inspiration, enlightenment, etc. as the term that signifies the absolute deity of Jesus which is of a different kind than the presence of God as Spirit in other people, it undermines the gospel of God's Reign which Jesus preached and lived.[51]

Accordingly, one may label Newman's Christology a Spirit-Christology of inspiration, for it is God as Spirit in Jesus who inspired an exemplary life of commitment to God's Reign that is paradigmatic for his followers today.

In some ways it is natural to turn now to James D. G. Dunn's Spirit-Christology,[52] for it has some similarities to Newman's; both focus on the relational/inspirational aspect of Jesus and God as underscored by the presence of the Spirit in him. Dunn's position is clearly stated in his succinct and conclusive summaries. In his book on *Jesus and the Spirit*, he comments,

> Certainly it is quite clear that if we can indeed properly speak of the "divinity" of the *historical* Jesus, we can only do so in terms of his experience of God: *his "divinity" means his relationship with the Father as son and the Spirit of God in him.*[53]

Significantly, Dunn is highly interested in Jesus' own view of his relationship to the Spirit, which he views mainly in terms of "inspiration and empowering."[54] The way he puts the two together is by proposing a two-stage Spirit-Christology. The quotation above corresponds to the first stage, which focuses on the earthly life and ministry of Jesus and the Spirit's inspirational influence upon him. The second stage corresponds to the post-exaltation existence of Jesus, which Dunn understands as Jesus becoming "Lord of the Spirit" through his resurrection from the dead.

51. Ibid.

52. Unlike the previous two scholars, James D. G. Dunn has been a dialogue partner with Pentecostal views from the beginning of his career, as can be seen from his articles and books that address Pentecostalism's understanding of the Spirit. For instance, his doctoral dissertation was entitled *Baptism in the Holy Spirit: A Re-examination of the New Testament Teaching on the Gift of the Spirit in Relation to Pentecostalism Today*.

53. Dunn, *Jesus and the Spirit*, 92; emphasis original.

54. Dunn, *Christology in the Making*, 138.

Central to Dunn's proposal for a two-stage Spirit-Christology is his understanding of Adam Christology, which for him is a major component of early Christians' quest to understand the significance of Jesus of Nazareth. For example, Dunn considers that Luke (possibly influenced by Paul) endorses an Adam Christology in his presentation of Jesus' baptism at the Jordan:

> It can hardly be an accident that Luke inserts the genealogy of Jesus between his anointing with the Spirit and his temptation, nor that he traces Jesus' family tree back to "Adam, Son of God." Here is the race of Adam, the son of God, a race, which, by implication, suffered through his fall. But here now is the second Adam, "the Adam of the End-time," newly hailed Son of God, who is led forth into the wilderness to do battle with the same Satan, and to reverse the tragic results of the Fall, first by refusing to succumb himself, and then by acting on fallen man's behalf.[55]

Significantly, though, Dunn makes it clear that when Paul speaks of the "second Adam" it is in reference to the Risen Christ, not Jesus in his human existence on earth. Moreover, "*Christ's role as second man, as last Adam, does not begin either in some pre-existent state, or at the incarnation, but at his resurrection.* For Paul, the resurrection marks the beginning of the representative humanity of the last Adam."[56] So what then becomes of the historical Jesus' earthly existence? This is why Dunn makes use of a two-stage Spirit-Christology.

Dunn attempts to argue for Jesus' full humanity and Christ's divine Sonship by distinguishing between the earthly Jesus and the exalted Christ. On the one hand, Jesus in his earthly life was as human as any other human being, to the point of sharing in humanity's fallen state. Yet, on the other hand, after his resurrection when Jesus became the Christ, he took on the role of divine Sonship. This two-stage Christology is affirmed, for Dunn, by early Christians' understanding of Psalm 8, specifically verses 4–6.

> [4] What is man that you are mindful of him,
>   and the son of man that you care for him?
> [5] You made him a little less then the angels,
>   and crowned him with glory and honor;

---

55. Dunn, *Baptism in the Holy Spirit*, 31.

56. Dunn, *Christology in the Making*, 108; emphasis original.

> ⁶ And you set him over the works of your hands,
>   having put all things in subjection under his feet.

In his reading of this passage, verses 4 and 5 are about the earthly Jesus and verse 6 speaks about his exalted state as the Christ.[57] Thus, there is a distinction between the "historical Jesus" and the "Christ of faith," although they are one and the same. So was Jesus purely human or also divine in his human manifestation?

For Dunn, the significance of Jesus' earthly life is particularly visible in his role as the "last Adam." He writes:

> The divine programme for man which broke down with Adam has been run through again with Jesus—this time successfully. It was by playing out the role of Adam that Christ became the last Adam: Adam led man to death and not glory; but Jesus by his life, suffering and death became the pioneer opening up the way through death for those who follow him (Heb 2:9).[58]

Thus, it is as the Risen Christ that Jesus is humankind's representative as the "last Adam." Dunn understands that Paul's theology gives a central place to Jesus' representative or corporative nature in comparison to that of Adam's.[59] For example, in Romans 5:12–21 and 1 Corinthians 15:20–23, 45–49, Paul compares and contrasts Jesus and Adam in such a way as to stress Christ's universal significance for human beings. In his understanding, just as Adam was a representative figure for all humans at all times, so Christ as the "last Adam" is able to bring life to believers.

Yet, whereas it is the resurrection that catapults Jesus into his representative status of "last Adam," it is his obedience as a human that enables him to become the Christ. And in order to accomplish this, from Dunn's perspective, Jesus had to completely identify with humanity to the point of sharing in its fallen nature. Dunn explains:

> It is generally agreed that "flesh" in Paul is not something evil in itself, but denotes man in his weakness and corruptibility. "Sinful flesh" means therefore not sin-committing flesh, but flesh under the dominion of sin (cf. Rom 6:6; 7:14)—that is, man in his

---

57. Dunn also argues that this exegetical insight is very plausibly pre-Pauline and the author of Hebrews interprets the passage just as he does. Ibid., 110.

58. Ibid.

59. Ibid., 101.

fallenness, man dominated by his merely human appetites and desires and in bondage to death (cf. 7:5). So whatever δμοίωμα means exactly, the phrase "precise likeness of sinful flesh" must denote Jesus in his oneness with sinful man, *in his complete identity with fallen Adam.*[60]

Thus, Dunn posits that Jesus' human nature was identical with Adam's fallen nature. Whatever distortion occurred in the humanity of Adam after the fall, Jesus was born in that same state. In a sense, following Dunn's logic, it is as if God ups the ante for the man Jesus: whereas Adam disobeyed in his pre-fallen state and as a result acquired an inferior status of sonship, Jesus is expected to become what God originally intended man to be from the fallen state, and not as Adam first had a chance to.

> The way in which Jesus becomes last Adam is by following the path taken by the first Adam. Christ starts his saving work by being one with Adam in his fallenness, before he becomes what Adam should have been. He follows in Adam's footsteps and at the point where Adam comes to an end in death he takes over and becomes what Adam did not become, *and no longer could become.* He becomes one with man in his falling shortness in order that through death and resurrection he might lift man to God's glory. He becomes one with man in his *sinfulness* in order that by the power of his life-giving Spirit he might remould man in God's righteousness. He becomes what Adam fell to by his disobedience in order that Adam might become what Christ was exalted to by his obedience.[61]

So how was Jesus able to overcome what Adam and his descendants could not? And how was he able to do it from a less advantageous position sharing in our human plight as fallen creatures?

Already in this last quotation Dunn announces the connection that he will later make between Jesus and the Spirit, which will establish how Jesus becomes and continues to be the Christ. After establishing that Christology cannot be understood in three stages where the third is his pre-existent stage, Dunn explores the relation between Jesus and the Spirit and suggests that Jesus experienced the power of God, the

---

60. Ibid., 112; emphasis added.
61. Ibid., 113; emphasis added.

Spirit, in a unique and eschatological measure in his life.[62] According to Dunn, Jesus of Nazareth was a man inspired by the Spirit like no one else, and it was this that enabled him to have success where the former Adam failed. Thus, it is because Jesus lived a life "according to the Spirit" that his life is more than merely a pattern to be followed, but truly the Savior of fallen humanity. On the phrase "according to the Spirit," Dunn explains:

> It is possible that Paul meant that Jesus' installation as Son of God (in power) "according to the Spirit" was in part at least the consequence of his having lived "according to the Spirit." It is certainly true that for Paul believers' hope of sharing in the resurrection, of a spiritual body (body of the Spirit), was at least to some extent dependent on their living according to the Spirit now (Rom 8:6, 11, 13, 23; Gal 6:8); and Paul did regard Jesus' resurrection as the archetype of believers' resurrection (Rom 8:11; 1 Cor 15:20–23). So he could have intended his readers that Jesus' pre-resurrection life was similarly archetypal—that Jesus, as sharing Adam's lot, nevertheless showed Adam the way to last Adam-(resurrection)-humanity in the Spirit, by himself living according to the Spirit.[63]

What characterizes Dunn's Spirit-Christology is a two-stage relation to Jesus, with the first stage being the Spirit inspiring and empowering Jesus in order to guide him in his conquest over against the human condition of fallenness. The second stage, to which we now turn, begins after the resurrection when Jesus becomes Lord of the Spirit. In short, the one previously *inspired by* the Spirit becomes the *dispenser of* the Spirit.[64]

With the aim of showing how Jesus becomes the bestower of the Spirit, Dunn adds an interesting caveat to previous models of Spirit-Christology: he equates the Spirit with the risen Jesus, the Christ.[65] This is significant because in a sense it completes the cycle of non-incarnational Spirit-Christologies by following God's presence as Spirit before, during, and after the history of the man Jesus. But how does Dunn manage this convergence of Jesus and the Spirit? Does he mean a

---

62. Ibid., 148.

63. Ibid., 139.

64. Dunn, "Towards the Spirit of Christ," 13–14.

65. Dunn, *Jesus and the Spirit*, 325–26.

transmutation between Jesus and the Spirit where the first becomes the latter? Dunn explains it like this:

> The Jesus of history was, as it were, the funnel through which the whole course of salvation-history flowed, and it came out at the other end transformed in terms of Jesus and stamped with his character. Forevermore now, God is the Father of our Lord Jesus Christ, and the Spirit is the Spirit of Christ.
>
> In brief, Jesus has given personality to the Spirit—his personality. The impersonal Spirit, like the impersonal Logos, is now identified with Jesus and bears his personality. In other words, as the Spirit is the divinity of Jesus, so Jesus is the personality of the Spirit.[66]

Yet Dunn is careful to indicate that by this he does not mean a complete transference of person where one obliterates the other.

Significantly Dunn states that "Before the incarnation Logos and Spirit were hardly to be distinguished. After the incarnation the divinity of Jesus was a function of the Spirit. And after the resurrection the risen humanity of Jesus was a function of the Spirit."[67] A critical issue in understanding Dunn's logic is his view of the incarnation, which he understands as the incarnation of Wisdom, seen not as a being independent of God but rather as God's self-manifestation. Dunn elaborates:

> The point is that Christ is the *incarnation* of this Wisdom/Word. To speak of *Christ* as himself pre-existent, coming down from heaven, and so forth, has to be seen as metaphorical; otherwise it leads inevitably to some kind of polytheism—the Father as a person, just like Jesus was a person. Whereas, what a Wisdom/Word christology claims is that Jesus is the person/individual whom God's Word *became*.[68]

As such, Dunn proposes that the incarnation should not be understood as the descent of the Son of God, but simply as the "incarnation of God's self-revelation."[69] Thus, one should only speak of pre-existence in reference to God's own Wisdom, in the Hebraic sense of divine Wisdom embodied in the Torah.

---

66. Dunn, *Christ and the Spirit*, 2:52.

67. Dunn, "Rediscovering the Spirit," 52–53.

68. Dunn, *Christ and the Spirit*, 1:47.

69. Ibid.

Although it is not the purpose of this chapter to judge the legitimacy of these Spirit-Christologies, but simply to present their distinct orientations, it is appropriate at least to say something brief about their perceived shortcomings. First of all, Lampe's position is a result of a selective use of Scripture. In effect, he sweeps a lot of potentially significant christological material under the carpet by arguing for a mythological understanding of the New Testament authors, which in our day and age should just be bypassed. However, this sort of selective exegesis, which cuts out the unwanted material and leaves the raw data that is in accord with the author's view, is highly problematic.

The same could be said of Newman's proposal, but what I find more puzzling in his perspective is how he seems either to misunderstand Trinitarianism completely or willingly misrepresent it. He continually argues that Trinitarian theology proposes outright polytheism—that belief in the Trinity amounts to belief in three gods. However, it might be well to remind Newman that throughout church history Trinitarians have repeatedly been accused of this and have always defended their position either on biblical or theological grounds, rejecting any understanding that results in a position where three gods are worshipped.

For his part, Dunn's proposal is inconsistent in various respects. It seems to me that Dunn's view leads to the universal deification of humanity by means of the life of the Spirit. Does not the fact that Jesus was able to overcome his "fallen" state through the inspiration and empowering of the Spirit suggest that humans today in their fallen state have the capacity to overcome their situation and become what Jesus became? Dunn does argue that the Spirit was given to Jesus in a special measure, and for that matter only he is able to live "according to the Spirit" in such a way as to be the Giver of the Spirit. However, I find his logic flawed. When Adam transgressed against God, what was lost was the communion that he shared with God before the fall, and as a result death came to us all, not, as Dunn suggests, the bond with the Spirit that Jesus renews through his death and resurrection. Had the bond with the Spirit been lost, there could not be any manifestations of the Spirit as recorded in the Old Testament. Moreover, it is incoherent to insist on the one hand that it is only at the resurrection that the Risen Christ becomes the "last Adam" when his argument is that Jesus overcame the temptations Adam was unable to overcome. But if Jesus needed to overcome where Adam could not, is it not more reasonable to propose that Jesus' humanity was like Adam's before the fall, and not like ours after the fall?

Revisionist Models of Spirit-Christology: Haight and Schoonenberg

Moving to the second model of Spirit-Christology, we will briefly examine the proposals of Roger Haight and Piet Schoonenberg, which in my opinion advocate a revisionist approach. Although both Del Colle and Habets understand Haight as attempting to replace the traditional Logos Christology, it is significant to note how he himself views his proposal. First of all, he insists that Spirit-Christology should not be considered as being "in opposition to a Logos or Word christology but in contrast to it."[70] Haight sees the two not as diametrically opposed to each other, but as currents of thought that run parallel to each other. Haight comments further on this:

> The argument here, however, will not entail a consistent polemic against Logos Christology. The aim is to develop a positive and constructive account, one which only occasionally and for purposes of clarification contrast the position here with that of a Logos Christology. The point here is thus not to affirm that a Logos Christology has been or is wrong but to characterize a Christology that is more adequate to our situation.[71]

Moreover, in outlining the basic principles that must guide the construction of any Christology, he explicitly considers that it "must be faithful to the great christological councils of Nicaea and Chalcedon."[72] Later he explains further that the inclusive function of Spirit: "God as Spirit working in the life of Jesus can form the basis for multiple interpretations of him by explaining why he was the Wisdom of God who spoke and even represented God's Word."[73]

70. Haight, *Jesus, Symbol of God*, 445.

71. Haight, "Case for Spirit Christology," 259.

72. The methodological premises that he outlines are: (1) an apologetic style, (2) fidelity to the biblical languages, (3) fidelity to the christological councils, (4) intelligible and coherent, (5) response to contemporary problems, and (6) stimulus and empowerment of Christian life. Ibid., 260–61.

73. Ibid., 272.

In the end what pushes me to consider Haight's position as revisionist, but not in the sense of total replacement, is his consideration that "nothing less than God was at work in Jesus."[74] Put even more boldly, Haight later contrasts his view with the conciliar affirmations arrived at in Nicaea. He postulates, "there is nothing affirmed with the doctrine of Nicaea that cannot also be affirmed in terms of God as Spirit. God as Spirit is God and thus not less than God."[75] Whatever misgivings one might have about Haight's position, one must understand that he still considers it an in-house debate, for he attempts to remain under the christological umbrella provided by the church councils, although he perhaps stretches its canopy to the limit.

What is telling is that he admits that his method and point of departure is "from below," by which he means to highlight the history of Jesus in a way that is not "compromised by later interpretations."[76] In this light, Haight proposes a return to the New Testament sources of Christology, and from this perspective he finds that the biblical symbol of Spirit is able to enlighten our path toward a Christology that is more relevant for today. Concerning Jesus' own perception of the work of God as Spirit in his life, Haight comments:

> Jesus was aware that whatever power he exercised was to be attributed to God as Spirit at work through him, and that others recognized this in these terms. . . . This power of God as Spirit at work in the world is closely associated with the kingdom of God, and Jesus' sense of mission too is understood in terms of anointing and empowerment by the Spirit. The synoptics also lead one to understand the presence and action of God as Spirit in his life as the ground of Jesus' Sonship . . ."[77]

Interestingly, Haight also proposes a two-stage Spirit-Christology similar to that of Dunn. As with Dunn, the first stage consists in the work of God as Spirit in the life of Jesus, and the second stage in the identification of Jesus with the Spirit after his resurrection. Haight further states:

74. Ibid.
75. Ibid., 274.
76. Haight, *Jesus*, 447.
77. Ibid., 448.

In all of this one sees Jesus and the Spirit placed in close conjunction with each other. First, God as Spirit is at work in Jesus'
life, and, then, in the case of Jesus risen, the conjunction tends
toward identification. God as Spirit was at work in Jesus so that,
after his death, when he is experienced as alive and with God,
Jesus is still closely mixed up with the very experience of God as
Spirit in the early community.[78]

Yet whereas Dunn sees the activity of the Spirit in the life of Jesus as
an exclusive work intended solely for him, Haight considers it in an
inclusive way.

Haight proposes that the best metaphor to "express the insight of
how God is present to and at work in Jesus in a Spirit Christology is
empowerment."[79] Here he fleshes this out in more detail:

As in Rahner's theology of the Spirit as grace, God's Spirit is the
presence of God's personal self in such a way that it dynamically
empowers human freedom. God's presence and empowerment
does not *over*power, but precisely activates human freedom so
that it is enhanced and not taken over; Jesus' human existence is
fulfilled and not replaced. But this is not a three-stage christology; and God as Spirit is not present as the subject of Jesus' being
and action. This is a more dynamic, interactive conception that
can be expressed by language of a divine Logos or Spirit assum-
ing a human nature. This should also be construed as more than
a thin functional or "adverbial" presence of God to Jesus, and
truly an ontological presence, because where God acts, God is.
In this empowerment christology Jesus is the reality of God.[80]

The soteriological implications that Haight's Spirit-Christology contains are best understood in terms of this empowerment. For just as
Jesus was empowered in his life by God as Spirit, so too are believers
empowered to live. What Haight suggests is that "Jesus' ministry of the

78. Ibid., 450.

79. Ibid., 454.

80. As a footnote to these comments, Haight remarkably discloses a change in his
understanding. Previously, Haight had agreed with Lampe's view that Jesus was divine
"adverbially" because of the dynamic presence of God as Spirit. See Haight, "Case for
Spirit Christology," 275. More recently, however, he has come to "agree with the critique
of that idea by Schoonenberg ["Spirit Christology and Logos Christology," 365]. One
cannot separate God's being and function in such a way. Jesus *is* divine dialectically, because the presence of God as Spirit pervades his being and action." Haight, *Jesus*, 455.

reign of God mediates personal *and* social salvation."[81] Thus, in his Spirit-Christology, Haight proposes that Jesus not only identifies with our humanity but also becomes an example to be imitated. Significantly, this following of Jesus is not solely in terms of personal "holy" living, but also in terms of a socially responsible pursuit of the kingdom of God.

Another Spirit-Christology that has been highly scrutinized and even deemed by some as heretical is that proposed by Piet Schoonenberg. Although one could very well trace the development of Schoonenberg's christological proposal and how it has revised in view of direct scholarly and indirect ecclesiastical critique,[82] I will briefly present only an outline of his ideas as found in his last christological work, *Der Geist, das Wort, und der Sohn.*[83]

Central to Piet Schoonenberg's thesis is the idea that the Gospels contain not just one type of Christology but various forms of understanding the divinity and humanity of the person of Jesus. Among these early biblical proposals are found Logos Christology, Wisdom Christology, and Spirit-Christology, in no particular order of importance. Schoonenberg's argument is that the conflation of Wisdom Christology with Spirit-Christology paved the way for the prominence of Word/Logos Christology. Schoonenberg comments, "In the New Testament Spirit-Christology and that of the Logos are not found too distant from each other and it is possible that their point of union lies in a hidden current of Wisdom Christology."[84] Moreover, the identification of Spirit-Christology with Wisdom Christology takes place early in the church fathers, who, as we saw above, have the tendency to subsume both into a Word Christology by means of a Logos understanding.

Yet for Schoonenberg, Spirit-Christologies and Logos Christologies are not mutually exclusive, "but on the contrary they complement and enrich each other reciprocally."[85] The main difference between the

81. Haight, *Jesus*, 456.

82. For a provocative study that considers Roger Haight and Schoonenberg's proposals together, see Loewe, "Two Revisionist Christologies," 93–115. For a sketch of the development of Schoonenberg's Spirit-Christology, see O'Keefe, "Spirit Christology of Piet Schoonenberg," 116–40.

83. The source being used is the Spanish translation by Ramon Puig Massana already mentioned; see Schoonenberg, *El Espíritu, la Palabra y el Hijo.*

84. Ibid., 79; my translation.

85. Ibid., 93; my translation.

two is that whereas in a Logos Christology Jesus descends from God, in a Spirit-Christology Jesus ascends to God. Thus, says, Michael E. O'Keeeffe:

> The foundation of Schoonenberg's biblical Spirit christology or "Spirit-Logos" christology is the principle that everything said about Jesus Christ must be compatible with the claim that he was fully human. For example, Jesus must have experienced the same "growth, learning, seeking, conflicts, [and] temptations" we do.[86]

As one capable of such experience, Schoonenberg claims Jesus is our pioneer, because he has gone before us in the journey. Thus, Schoonenberg presents a Christology of becoming, in which Jesus becomes the Son of God. He explains, "In his complete human reality, Jesus is carried by the Word and driven by the Spirit. Both make Jesus into the Son of God, so that both Word and Spirit-christology, are of equal value as an explanation of the divine sonship of Jesus."[87]

Here the critics could argue that Schoonenberg has completely abandoned classical Christology, and in some respects they are right. But what is important to note is that Schoonenberg's proposal aims to revise traditional Trinitarian theology in light of his presentation of the full humanity of Jesus. Thus, in the last chapter of his book, he postulates a Trinitarian doctrine "in-becoming." Key for his conclusion is that just as Jesus becomes Son of God, God himself is "in-becoming" because of Jesus.

> Even for God, particularly for the Logos which is God, a new thing begins [in Jesus Christ]. This new reality is the being-human, by which the Logos stands among human beings on earth and remains a human being for all eternity. God's Word speaks as a human being, with human words and out of a human consciousness and amidst a human community of language and tradition. And he speaks thus to God himself. The Word [Wort] has become response [Antwort]: the crown of the Johannine prologue is [therefore] the high-priestly prayer [for now the Word] . . . speaks to the Father in the prayer of a human being, whom it has become, and in the sacrifice of his human life. Moreover, God speaks to us through the incarnate Word in a

---

86. O'Keeffe, "Spirit Christology of Piet Schoonenberg," 120.

87. Ibid., 125; translation of Schoonenberg, *Der Geist*, 112.

> love which was already suffering love previously but which is
> now a love right to death, a love in complete renunciation.[88]

Judging by Schoonenberg's overall aims and his consistent following of his methodology, one has to agree that although his proposal is innovative and seemingly departs from orthodox Christology, he is not seeking ultimately to displace Logos Christology but is interested in recovering Spirit-Christology, and builds on it beginning with the absolute humanity of Jesus.

Complementary Models of Spirit-Christology: Pinnock and Suurmond

The third model that I propose is a complementary approach to Spirit-Christology that goes hand in hand with a Logos Christology as traditionally understood. In order to examine the main tenets of this model and at the same time to make a connection to Pentecostal Spirit-Christology, I will consider the work of two scholars: a non-Pentecostal who is very sympathetic toward the movement, Clark Pinnock; and a Charismatic, Jean Jacques Suurmond. My treatment of this model is scant, for in large part the complementary models critique the previous replacement and revisionist models. It would be tangential to fully explain why these authors reject the previous models, although in many ways just from presenting their models their correctives will be apparent.

Clark Pinnock's proposal for Spirit-Christology departs from the notion of seeking to give the Holy Spirit a central place in the understanding of the life and ministry of Jesus Christ. The entry point for Pinnock is his conception of Jesus' anointing with the Spirit. Pinnock suggests that

> It was anointing by the Spirit that made Jesus "Christ," not the
> hypostatic union, and it was the anointing that made him effec-
> tive in history as the absolute Savior. Jesus was ontologically Son
> of God from the moment of conception, but he became Christ
> by the power of the Holy Spirit. When Satan tempted him to
> misuse his powers, the Son refused, choosing the path of depen-
> dence on the Spirit.[89]

88. Ibid. 130; translation of Schoonenberg, *Der Geist*, 127–28.

89. Pinnock, *Flame of Love*, 80.

From this quotation the main parameters of Pinnock's Spirit-Christology can already be ascertained. First, the Spirit-Christology proposed by Pinnock is complementary to a Logos Christology and does not seek to replace it. In a sense, Pinnock wants to establish the role of the Spirit in the life of Jesus, but without rejecting an incarnational Christology. Moreover, he maintains the notion of the hypostatic union as key for comprehending Jesus' deity as ontologically the same as God. Thus, at the time of conception the Logos became incarnate in the human person of Jesus.

Second, Pinnock highlights Jesus' anointing of the Spirit at the Jordan as the event in which Jesus becomes the Christ. What is peculiar about Pinnock's proposal is that although he understands that "it was by the Spirit that Jesus was conceived," and not just "anointed, empowered, commissioned, directed and raised up," it is surprising that he does not consider Jesus to have been "anointed" at conception, rather than at his baptism.[90] In part this is because Pinnock understands the Spirit to have been acting since the beginning of creation.

The mission of the Spirit, thus understood, does not begin at Pentecost, but it can be traced back through the Old Testament and indeed to the foundation of the world. Pinnock insists that "redemption through Jesus is an action of the Spirit of life actualizing the original creation purposes of God."[91] Instead of a linear view of salvation history, Pinnock opts for an overarching view where the mission of the Son takes place under the larger umbrella of the mission of the Spirit. As active agent of God's redemptive purposes, the Spirit anoints the Son who was "conscious of a joint operation with the Spirit" in fulfilling God's salvific purposes. Still, why does Jesus become the Christ at his baptism and not from his birth? To complicate matters even more, Pinnock notes that Jesus was "already anointed by the Spirit as Christ in Mary's womb."[92] The difference is that at his baptism the Spirit came upon Jesus with power.[93] Jesus' baptism in the Spirit meant "he was endowed with power and equipped for mission."[94] What followed his baptism was a time of

90. Ibid., 81–82.
91. Ibid., 83.
92. Ibid., 86.
93. Ibid.
94. Ibid., 87.

testing where Jesus, as representative of the human race, would have to face and conquer the temptations that Adam could not overcome. The Spirit gave Jesus wisdom in order to overcome. Furthermore, it was Jesus' complete dependence on the Spirit that enabled him to obtain the victory.

Pinnock also suggests that Jesus' human nature was in the likeness of sinful flesh, a fallen nature. In this state, Jesus' sinlessness was not on account of his own deity but through his relation with the Spirit. Pinnock makes it clear that "in becoming dependent, the Son surrendered the independent use of his divine attributes in incarnation. The Word became flesh and exercised power through the Spirit, not on its own."[95] Thus, in God's infinite purposes was the plan for the Son to become human and "live a life of obedience in the power of the Spirit" in order that through his resurrection humanity also would be able to participate in the new creation.[96] Accordingly, Pinnock sees a reciprocal relationship between what Jesus was able to accomplish through his life in the Spirit and the believers' union with Christ in and through the Spirit.

Charismatic Jean Jacques Suurmond in his doctoral dissertation proposes a different way of developing a Spirit-Christology. He suggests that an exclusive approach to Spirit-Christology that rejects a Logos Christology is wrongheaded because of how it affects Trinitarian thought.[97] Yet Suurmond suggests that a Logos Christology and a Spirit-Christology are not mutually exclusive:

> Both strands are found in the New Testament, and both must be held together in any interpretation of the Christ-event. A Word christology starts "from above" and is concerned with the incarnatio, addressing the question of what it means for God to become man. A Spirit christology, on the other hand, starts "from below" and focuses on the incarnatum, i.e. the historical event that was Jesus of Nazareth. Both are valid and needed as they complement each other in the attempt to interpret the phenomenon of Jesus the God-man.[98]

95. Ibid., 88.

96. Ibid., 97.

97. Suurmond, "Ethical Influence," 375.

98. Ibid., 375–76.

Suurmond characterizes this complementary notion of Logos Christology and Spirit-Christology by seeing both working together in the life and ministry of Jesus Christ.

Leaning heavily on the Hebrew understanding of Wisdom, Suurmond grounds his Spirit-Christology in an Old Testament framework. Quoting from Proverbs 8:22–31, Suurmond introduces Wisdom as a lady:

> Yahweh created me at the beginning of his work
> . . . when he laid the foundations of the earth
> then I was with him as the apple of his eye
> and I was daily his joy;
> constantly playing before his face,
> playing in his inhabited world
> and rejoicing in the children of men.

Moreover, Suurmond comments that "the book of Proverbs opens with an introduction from which it emerges that in Lady Wisdom there is both a 'spirit' which she wants to pour out, and 'words' with which she calls loudly in the streets."[99] Accordingly, Word and Spirit come together in the concept of Wisdom. An analogy that is helpful for understanding the idea that Suurmond develops is that in Scripture both Word and Spirit are "always thought of together."[100] In a sense, the first provides order while the second provides dynamism. Like yin and yang, both "Word and Spirit are present at every level of creation, and work towards the eternal Sabbath which has already become visible in a unique way in a man from Nazareth."[101]

According to Suurmond, in the New Testament there is a coalescence between Lady Wisdom and Jesus. For example, the hymn of Colossians 1:15–20 states that Jesus is "the image of the invisible God" (v 15) and that "in him all things in heaven and on earth were created" (v. 16). This echoes the Wisdom of Solomon's description of wisdom as "a pure emanation of the glory of the Almighty" (7:25) and Proverbs' understanding of wisdom as the foundation of all things (3:19). In addition, Suurmond provides an extended comparison of the parallels

99. Suurmond, *Word and Spirit at Play*, 38.

100. Ibid., 40.

101. Ibid., 41.

between Lady Wisdom and Jesus.[102] Thus, instead of opting for either a Word/Logos Christology or a Spirit-Christology exclusively, Suurmond proposes that "only a Wisdom christology, one in which both Word and Spirit are honoured, does complete justice to the person of Jesus."[103]

In this respect, then, it is better to think of John's Logos from a Hebrew perspective like that of Philo's, who understood it both in terms of "the creative Word of God and personified Wisdom," and not just the "all-pervading ordering principle of the Stoics."[104] After all, Jesus identifies himself and his ministry with playful Wisdom in Luke 7:31–35, where he gives an interesting analogy between his and John the Baptist's ministries by underscoring that although one invited the people to lament and the other to dance, neither promptings were heeded.

> "To what then will I compare the people of this generation, and what are they like? They are like children sitting in the market-place and calling to one another,
> 'We played the flute for you, and you did not dance;
> we wailed, and you did not weep.'
> For John the Baptist has come eating no bread and drinking no wine, and you say, 'He has a demon'; the Son of Man has come eating and drinking, and you say, 'Look, a glutton and a drunkard, a friend of tax collectors and sinners!'" (Luke 7:31–34)

Suurmond sees this passage as Jesus' own understanding of the rejection of John the Baptist's ministry as well as his own. Even more illuminating for Suurmond is Jesus' culminating saying, which seems to indicate Jesus' self-identification with Lady Wisdom: "Nevertheless, wisdom is vindicated by all her children" (v. 35).

In a sense, then, what Suurmond wants to get across is that Logos/Word Christology and Spirit-Christology, whatever their exact origins, need to be seen as two sides of the same coin, namely, a Wisdom Christology. In contrast to those who try to pit one Christology against the other, Suurmond suggests that the two illumine one another reciprocally.

---

102. Ibid., 43.
103. Ibid., 45.
104. Ibid., 46.

The Pentecostal Turn to Spirit-Christology

One might say that the Pentecostal turn toward Spirit-Christology is still under way, for many more proposals have been floated than the ones here mentioned. Sadly, most of these proposals are still in fragmentary and embryonic form and have not yet been fully developed.[105] Take for example the seminal comments that Frank D. Macchia makes in his highly acclaimed work *Baptized in the Spirit*. Fundamentally understanding Jesus as the Baptizer in the Spirit, Macchia rightly highlights that "Jew and Gentile were originally united by their faith in Jesus as the Spirit Baptizer."[106] He further comments, "It is God the Son as the Spirit Baptizer that became the unique link between the Father and the Spirit and, indirectly, to the doctrine of the Trinity."[107] Such theologically pregnant comments beg for a full-scale construction of a Spirit-Christology in light of the baptism of the Holy Spirit.

Establishing the Parameters

Some helpful guidelines toward the construction of such a Spirit-Christology are developed by Myk Habets. The first principle he outlines is that Spirit-Christology should seek to maintain "the twin concepts of both the filiological and the pneumatological aspects of Christology."[108] In a sense, one's theological outlook must keep one eye on the relationship between Jesus and the Father, while at the same time observing what happens in the relationship between Jesus and the Spirit. Thus, a serious Pentecostal Spirit-Christology must keep the interrelationships of the Trinity always in mind.

Second, the approach must be a thoroughly Scriptural account of Spirit-Christology that aims to test the functionality and interpenetration of the Trinitarian relationships. Succinctly put, "all three persons of the Trinity, within their relationships, help constitute each other."[109]

---

105. While making the final touches to this manuscript, I was pleasantly surprised by the publication of a book in this series, which would have made a valuable contribution to this work. Myk Habets, *The Anointed Son: A Trinitarian Spirit-Christology*. PTMS 129. Eugene, OR: Wipf & Stock, 2010.

106. Macchia, *Baptized in the Spirit*, 109.

107. Ibid., 110.

108. Habets, "Spirit Christology," 229.

109. Ibid., 231.

Essentially, then, the contours of a Spirit-Christology need to stay within the Trinitarian structure of Pentecostal beliefs.

Recent Pentecostal Proposals

Two interesting working proposals for Spirit-Christology from a Pentecostal perspective are those of Amos Yong and S. D. L. Jenkins. I qualify them as "working proposals" because of their incipient or preliminary nature. As such, it is possible only to sketch the main thrust of their arguments lest I misrepresent their proposals.

Amos Yong's proposal stems from his perception that "pneumatology is central to a robustly Trinitarian vision of God."[110] One governing principle of Yong's Spirit-Christology is the Irenaean concept of the "two hands of the Father" (Irenaeus *Haer.* 4.20.1). Another principle is the idea of *perichoresis*, which Yong understands as the "mutuality of partners in a dance."[111] Yong proposes that "the divine persons are understood not as individuals in the modern sense of personhood, but as relationships in the perichoretic sense of the mutuality of partners in a dance."[112] From this perspective, Yong conceives the Spirit as "the mutual love between the Father and the Son."[113] It is in this direction that Yong intends to remedy the opposition between a Logos Christology on the one hand and a Spirit-Christology on the other; instead they are mutually penetrating missions of the Trinitarian God.

In his most recent book, Yong sketches his relational Trinitarian Spirit-Christology from a biblical and Pentecostal perspective, mining the motif of Jesus the Christ—the anointed One—from a thoroughly pneumatological perspective. Yong argues that Luke intends to substantiate the claim that "if the Spirit of God who anointed Jesus dwells in you, the Spirit will empower you to do the same works (Acts) that Jesus did under the same anointing (Luke)."[114] Thus, the impetus of Yong's delineations is in effect to establish a paradigmatic functionality for understanding Spirit-Christology from a Pentecostal viewpoint.

---

110. Yong, *Spirit-Word-Community*, 49.

111. Ibid., 53.

112. Ibid., 56.

113. Ibid., 59.

114. Yong, *Spirit Poured Out*, 88.

S. D. L. Jenkins's preliminary sketch for a Spirit-Christology comes at the end of his dissertation. He builds on the insights of Edward Irving, James D. G. Dunn, and David Coffey, proposing that early Pentecostals understood the fall as the loss of the Holy Spirit. Moreover, following Dunn, Jenkins insists that Pentecostals can benefit from an understanding of Jesus' humanity where he assumes our fallen state and not Adam's pre-fall nature. In that state, Jesus Christ's obedience to the Father was accomplished through his responsiveness to the Holy Spirit, much as the Spirit's function in the believer is to sanctify us by empowering our own obedience. Here the reader only needs to be reminded of the critique of Dunn's Spirit-Christology above, for Jenkins seems to follow in his lead.[115]

The Oneness View of Jesus: A Test Case for Pentecostal Spirit-Christology

If Spirit-Christology is a viable model for a Pentecostal Christology, than not only must it be able to highlight the distinctives of classical Pentecostal beliefs, it must also serve as a tool for dialogue. Whereas for the most part two different Pentecostal movements (Trinitarian and Oneness Pentecostals) have existed in opposition since their split, it serves as a case in point to test out the strength of Spirit-Christology as a dialogical model. Here I will follow David K. Bernard's recent book *The Oneness View of Jesus Christ*, where he defends the official position of the United Pentecostal Church International,[116] and then offer some preliminary observations of the usefulness of Spirit-Christology for one of Pentecostalism's most controversial internal discussions.

---

115. For a recent analysis that offers a corrective to Dunn's Adam Christology and insists that the major difference between the first and second Adam was that the latter was able to do what the former could not, mainly avoid falling into sin, see Fee, *Pauline Christology*, 513–29.

116. The United Pentecostal Church International is the largest Oneness Pentecostal church body today, with over two million members worldwide. Hall, "United Pentecostal Church."

The Oneness Pentecostal View of Jesus

Bernard begins his presentation by succinctly stating Oneness doctrine by "two affirmations: 1) There is one God with no distinction of persons; 2) Jesus Christ is all the fullness of the Godhead incarnate."[117] The Oneness view of God is uncompromisingly monotheistic, finding no essential distinction in God's eternal divine nature. As a result, any talk of "Trinity" or of "persons in the Godhead" is automatically rejected on grounds that it is unbiblical and contrary to the Oneness doctrine of God found in the Old and New Testaments.[118] In seeking to maintain this absolute monotheism, Bernard's understanding of Jesus' deity is given special consideration. What does it mean to say, "Jesus Christ is the one God incarnate?"[119]

Essentially, Oneness Pentecostals believe that Jesus is "the incarnation of all the identity, character, and personality of the one God," and not, as Trinitarian theology affirms, the incarnation of the second person of the Trinity.[120] Bernard finds Scriptural support for his position in Colossians 2:9, which states, "for in the whole fullness of deity dwells bodily." Such a position results in the assertion of four bold conclusions: (1) Jesus cannot be anyone other than Yahweh, the God of the Old Testament; (2) in Jesus the Father (God) became incarnate; (3) the Holy Spirit is the same Spirit that was in Jesus; and 4) Jesus is the One sitting on the throne.

At first glance, one might label these declarations as expressing a sort of modern-day modalism because they understand God's manifestations throughout history as different modes of the one divine person of God. For example, Allen Anderson concludes, "Oneness Pentecostals hold that Jesus is the revelation of God the Father and that the Spirit

---

117. Bernard, *Oneness View of Jesus Christ*, 9.

118. In addition, Bernard wrongly accuses Trinitarians of being tritheists. He defines tritheism as: "Belief in three gods. As such, it is a form of polytheism. Advocates of trinitarianism deny that they are tritheists; however, trinitarianism certainly has tritheistic tendencies and some extreme forms of trinitarianism are tritheistic. For example, any belief that there are three self-conscious minds in the Godhead or three eternal bodies in the Godhead can properly be called tritheism." Bernard, *The Oneness of God*, 325.

119. Bernard, *Oneness View of Jesus Christ*, 12.

120. Ibid.

proceeds from the Father (Jesus)."[121] Thus, "Jesus" is the name of God in the New Testament and Father, Son and Holy Spirit are "modes" or "manifestations" of the singular God. Significantly, this label is not rejected wholly by Oneness Pentecostals, for Bernard agrees that "modalism upholds the same essentials as the modern doctrine of Oneness."[122] Yet, Bernard is quick to distinguish his position from any form of modalism that does not teach the full deity of Jesus Christ.

For example, he steers away from "dynamic monarchianism," because it "upheld the Oneness of God but did so by claiming that Jesus was an inferior, subordinate being."[123] Moreover, Bernard also rejects the teaching of Sabellius, who taught successive revelation (or manifestation) of God in history; first as Father, then the Son, and lastly as the Spirit.[124] The sort of modalism that Bernard opts for is what has been labeled "modalistic monarchianism." Thus he defines his own modalist doctrine (and that of the Oneness movement) as "the belief that the Father, Son, and Holy Ghost are only manifestations, or *modes*, of the one God (the *monarchia*) and not three distinct persons (*hypostases*)."[125]

This overarching understanding of God's Oneness prompts questions concerning the nature of Jesus and the exact meaning of his deity. To begin, Oneness Pentecostals believe that Jesus is God in the sense that he is the one and only Savior as spoken of both in the Old and New Testaments. Thus, the God that the Jews came to know in the Old Testament manifested himself in the flesh as Jesus; God himself, and not a person within the Godhead, took on human flesh.[126] But then, how are the descriptors "Father" and "Son" understood by Oneness Pentecostals?

---

121. Anderson, *Introduction to Pentecostalism*, 50.

122. The full definition that Bernard gives for the term "modalism" is: "Term used to describe a belief in early church history that Father, Son, and Spirit are not eternal distinctions within God's nature but simply *modes* (methods or manifestations) of God's activity. In other words, God is one individual being, and various terms used to describe him (such as Father, Son, and Holy Spirit) are designations applied to different forms of his action or different relationships He has to humans." Bernard, *Oneness of God*, 318.

123. Ibid., 248.

124. Ibid., 240.

125. Ibid., 248.

126. Ibid., 58.

The use of parental language does not necessarily denote intra-Trinitarian relationships where the Father is one person of the Trinity and the Son another. Bernard affirms that

> the titles of Father, Son, and Holy Spirit describe God's redemptive roles or revelations, but they do not reflect an essential threeness in His nature. Father refers to God in family relationship to humanity; Son refers to God in flesh; and Spirit refers to God in spiritual activity. For example, one man can have three significant relationships or functions—such as administrator, teacher, and counselor—and yet be one person in every sense. God is not defined by or limited to an essential threeness.[127]

Thus, there is no filial relationship between the Father and the Son as expressed by these human terms. If anything, "the Holy Spirit is literally the Father of Jesus, since Jesus was conceived by the Holy Spirit (Matt 1:18, 20)."[128] Again, this refers not to a filial relationship, but to the activity of God as Spirit begetting the human body of Jesus.

According to Oneness belief, Jesus the human manifestation of God had a beginning: the incarnation. At a specific point in time, Jesus, "the physical expression of the one God," came to existence "when the Spirit of God miraculously caused conception to take place in the womb of Mary."[129] What this means is that Jesus Christ did not exist prior to his incarnation, though God existed as Father and Holy Spirit. Furthermore, when "Jesus walked on earth as God himself incarnate the Spirit of God continued to be omnipresent."[130] A helpful metaphor for understanding this idea is to compare the Godhead to a wheel where the central hub is Jesus (the physical manifestation of God) and God (the omnipresent Spirit) is the rest of the wheel. Both the human (Jesus) and divine (Spirit) natures constitute the essence of the One God, each having specific functions.

---

127. Bernard, *Oneness View of Jesus Christ*, 16.

128. Ibid., 16–17.

129. Bernard, *Oneness of God*, 99, 104.

130. Bernard, *Oneness View of Jesus Christ*, 15.

Spirit-Christology as a Model for Oneness Pentecostal Christology

Considering the nature of the person of Jesus Christ, the Oneness position also affirms a two-natures doctrine, but in a way that is quite different from a Chalcedonian approach. Since Oneness scholars deny the pre-existence of Jesus, either as Logos or the Son, the nature of the person of Jesus is considered from the incarnation forward. Specifically referring to the dual nature of Christ, Bernard comments,

> From the Bible we see that Jesus Christ had two distinct natures in a way that no other human being has ever had. One nature is human or fleshly; the other nature is divine or Spirit. Jesus was both fully man and fully God. The name *Jesus* refers to the eternal Spirit of God (the Father) dwelling in the flesh. We can use the name *Jesus* when describing either aspect or both. For example, when we say Jesus died on the cross, we mean His flesh died on the cross. When we say Jesus lives in our hearts, we mean his Spirit is there.[131]

In speaking of the two natures of Christ from a Oneness perspective, then, it is not meant that the eternal and pre-existent Son of God became incarnate as the man Jesus. Rather, God the eternal Spirit incarnated himself in the person of Jesus Christ. Therefore, although Christ's deity needs to be distinguished from his humanity, it is not possible to separate them. "[Jesus'] human spirit and His divine Spirit were inseparable: in fact, it may be more proper to speak of the human aspect and the divine aspect of His one Spirit."[132] Significantly, then, the best way to understand Oneness Christology is by understanding God the Spirit as intrinsically joined to the humanity of Jesus, which presumably is best expressed by the model of Spirit-Christology.

If my thinking is correct then, it is more likely that dialogue between Trinitarian Pentecostals and Oneness Pentecostals may ensue from a Spirit-Christology perspective where the two Christologies overlap. Thus, by reflecting on the meaning of the presence and power of the Spirit in the life of Jesus, intra-Pentecostal christological dialogue might find a more fruitful harvest and mutual understanding.

131. Bernard, *Oneness of God*, 86.
132. Bernard, *Oneness View of Jesus Christ*, 21.

3

Latin American and Latina/o Christologies

THE PREVIOUS TWO CHAPTERS DEMONSTRATED HOW RECOVERY OF the distinctive features of early Pentecostal Christology is made more feasible by the adoption of Spirit-Christology as a paradigm, which is more in line with Pentecostalism's pneumatological orientation. Not only is Spirit-Christology a viable model for Trinitarian Pentecostals, but Oneness Pentecostals could also profit from such an approach. Yet, when one considers the social context of Hispanics in the U.S., one might wonder if this model is really able to be relevant to their specific needs. Does Spirit-Christology provide an applicable paradigm that addresses the main concerns of Hispanic Pentecostals, that is, of the people themselves, rather than any theological viewpoint supposed to be held by them?

In considering the various models of Spirit-Christology surveyed in the last chapter, it becomes clear that appropriating the paradigm requires a shift in methodology, specifically a Spirit-Christology from a contextual and liberative perspective. Later in this chapter, I explain in detail the rationale for such a move, for now I will simply say that it concerns the reality of the Hispanic Pentecostal church. To speak of the Hispanic Pentecostal church is to speak of the poor who live in the Spirit. For given the social location of the majority of Pentecostal churches in the U.S.—the *barrios* (ghettoes)—it is imperative that their theology reflect not only the Pentecostal imagination, but also the social dimensions of the people they seek to serve. In light of this, this chapter will survey Latin American and Latina/o Christologies as models for doing theology from a liberative and contextual perspective. The purpose of this chapter, then, is to orient Spirit-Christology toward a liberative perspective that is relevant for Hispanic Pentecostals.

Latin American Liberation Christology: Opting for the Crucified

Latin American liberation theology arose from the notion that all theological reflection departs from a particular social and ecclesial setting. There is no such thing as a free-floating theological endeavor, no theologizing about the person and work of Jesus Christ without regard to social and ecclesial function. As Boff puts it:

> Theologians do not live in the clouds. They are social actors with a particular place in society. They produce knowledge, data, and meanings by using instruments that the situation offers them and permits them to utilize. Their findings are also addressed to a particular audience. Thus theologians are framed within the overall social context. The themes and emphases of a given Christology flow from what seems relevant to the theologian on the basis of his or her social standpoint. In that sense we must maintain that no Christology is or can be neutral. Every Christology is partisan and committed. Willingly or unwillingly Christological discourse is voiced in a given social setting with all the conflicting interests that pervade it.[1]

The first distinction in the methodology of liberation Christology, therefore, is its deliberate recognition of the specific place from which its theological thought springs. Instead of claiming a supposed objectivity, it openly admits to being a subjective discourse about the life, message, and work of Jesus seen from the immediate context of Latin America.

Liberation theologians seek to liberate Christology from a purely academic and theoretical foreground, and explore its praxic dimensions for the sake of the oppressed living in Latin America. Thus, behind the methodology and content of liberation Christology, there are ideologies or hermeneutics that govern how and why the person and work of Jesus will be studied. In his book *Christology, a Global Introduction*, Veli-Matti Kärkkäinen summarizes the hermeneutic proposed by liberation theologians. He suggests it includes:

1. Ideological suspicion: an emerging notion that perhaps something is wrong in society, especially among the underprivileged.

---

1. Boff, *Jesus Christ Liberator*, 265.

2.   Analytical reflection on the social-value system: asking penetrating questions such as whether a situation is justified by Scripture and whether God's purposes are fulfilled in it.

3.   Exegetical suspicion: an acknowledgment of the fact that theology is not relevant because of a one-sided and biased style of reading the Bible that neglects the perspective of the poor and the oppressed.

4.   Pastoral action: articulating an appropriate response to what is determined to be one's personal biblical responsibility.[2]

Through an ongoing dialogue with these premises, liberation theologians guide their theological work, which aims to be liberative in its nature.

This was not, however, a new hermeneutic for Latin America, nor necessarily a new way of doing theology; in fact, ever since the coming of the gospel to Latin American continents, there has been a subversive attitude toward the injustices committed in the name of Christ against the indigenous cultures that lived in the Americas during the conquest. Against the ideology that the Spanish conquistadors were the bearers of Christ and the gospel, Fray Bartolomé de Las Casas articulated a most revolutionary statement: "Christ speaks to us from the Indians!"[3] Moreover, Las Casas identified the suffering of the Indians with the sufferings of Christ and protested against the cruelties of the Spaniards. He declared, "In the Indies I leave Jesus Christ, our God, being whipped and afflicted, and buffeted and crucified, not once but thousands of times, as often as the Spaniards assault and destroy those people."[4]

In this vein, the reflections of Miguel de Unamuno (1864–1936) on the painting of Diego Velázquez (1599–1660), "The Spanish Christ,"[5] and the recumbent Christ found in the *Iglesia de la Cruz* in Palencia[6]

2. Kärkkäinen, *Christology, a Global Introduction*, 225.

3. Cook, "Jesus from the Other Side of History," 259.

4. Quoted in Gutiérrez, *Dios o el Oro en las Indias*, 156.

5. Padilla comments, "the Christ of popular religiosity [in the Americas] was the dead Jesus, defeated and helpless, eloquently portrayed by Velázquez." Padilla, "Toward a Contextual Christology," 82.

6. Whereas Velázquez' painting of the crucified Christ depicts him as dying, in the Christ of Palencia he lies "cradled in the arms of Franciscan nuns, he is dead forever. He has become the incarnation of death itself." Mackay, *Other Spanish Christ*, 97.

capture the complete dissatisfaction with which the imported Christ of Spain was met by the indigenous population of the Americas. Writing centuries later but reflecting on the religious environment that the Spanish conquest produced, Unamuno wrote:

> This Spanish Christ who has never lived, black as the mantle of the earth, lies horizontal and stretched out like a plain, without soul and without hope, with closed eyes facing heaven. . . . And the poor Franciscan nuns of the Convent in which the Virgin Mother served—the Virgin of all heaven and life, gone back to heaven without having passed through death—cradle the death of the terrible Christ who will not awake upon earth. For he, the Christ of my land (tierra) is only dirt (tierra), dirt, dirt, dirt, . . . flesh, which does not palpitate, dirt, dirt, dirt, dirt . . . clots of blood which does not flow, dirt, dirt, dirt, dirt.
>
> And Thou, Christ of Heaven, redeem us from the Christ of earth (tierra).[7]

The Christ whom the conquistadors brought to the Americas was "a Christ unable to respond to the cries of the poor, a symbol of their passivity in the face of their oppressors."[8]

The seeds for the ideology proposed by liberation theologians have therefore been present in Latin America ever since the conquest.[9] In a manner similar to Las Casas and Unamuno, and with the aim of giving Latin America an indigenous Christology, liberation theologians adopted a new methodology, born from the lived experience of those who have been under oppression since the conquest of the Americas.

The Methodology of Liberation Christology

Liberation Christology seeks to "sketch a new image of Jesus Christ the Liberator" beginning with the hermeneutical locus of "the option for the poor and their cause."[10] It alleges, from the perspective of the poor in Latin America, to venture into theological contemplation on the per-

---

7. Miguel de Unamuno, "El Cristo Yacente de Santa Clara de Palencia"; quoted in Mackay, *Other Spanish Christ*, 98.

8. Padilla, "Toward a Contextual Christology," 82.

9. Other studies on "Christologies of conquest" that solidify this premise can be found in the following sources: Pagán, *Violent Evangelism*; Trinidad, "Christology, Conquista, Colonization"; and Assmann, "Power of Christ in History."

10. Lois, "Christology in the Theology of Liberation," 170.

son of Jesus that will result in liberative meaning for the oppressed and produce structural change in society. It is precisely because liberation theologians recognize their theological place for doing Christology as "the world of the poor" that affinities with the social structures present in Jesus' time are brought into their christological understanding. Yet, are the poor a legitimate theological locus from which to examine and comprehend the person and work of Jesus?

Reflecting on the "world of the poor" as a theological locus for Christology, Hugo Assmann writes:

> If the state of domination and dependence in which two-thirds of humanity live, with an annual toll of thirty million dead from starvation and malnutrition, does not become the starting point for *any* Christian theology today, even in the affluent and powerful countries, then theology will be unable to give any historical context or content to its basic themes.[11]

Sobrino further defends "the option for the poor" as a central place from which to do theology, arguing that it makes theological reflection relevant:

> This is also what stimulates Christological thinking and gives it a basic direction: to think about Christ from the perspective of the fact of real life and death, to relate him to the basic needs of the poor, to present Christ as the word of life in the presence of anti-life, as someone who came to bring life, life to the full.[12]

Moreover, since theology surges from the faith of a church community, this new christological portrait is drawn from a distinct ecclesial locus: the church of the poor. If the "world of the poor" is a concrete reality in our world, then the church cannot simply close her eyes with regard to their material and spiritual needs. Following in the footsteps of her founder, the church continues his ministry to the poor, becoming the church of the poor. What characterizes the church of the poor is her willingness to be and act as Jesus. Thus, in order for a complete consideration of Jesus Christ, liberation theologians seek to encounter those in whom Jesus has chosen to continue to manifest his presence in his-

---

11. Assmann, *Teología Desde la Praxis de la Liberación*, 40. With relation to the significance of the liberative perspective for a global theology, see Kärkkäinen, *Christology*, 226.

12. Sobrino, *Jesus the Liberator*, 32.

tory (the poor; see Matt 25:31–46) and to put Jesus' actions toward the poor into practice within the church.

It is in the intersection of the social and the ecclesial that a Christology of liberation has its origin. Accordingly, for liberation theologians the task of thinking theologically about Jesus does not begin in the abstract reflection of classical christological formulations. The *first act* is the following of Jesus, "making the same option for the poor and their cause that he made, and translating this option, in current circumstances, into a commitment to a liberative transformation of reality."[13] The *second act* is the reflection that results in light of the faith that is born out of being a disciple of Jesus. In other words, it is through a life of discipleship, the following in the steps of Jesus who makes his cause that of the poor, that believers can come to know him. Put more concisely, "to know Jesus is to follow him."[14]

The consequence of elaborating theology in this manner is the development of the praxic dimension of theology. Liberation theology seeks not merely to be involved in the interpretive process, but boldly attempts to influence and transform the oppressive realities that operate in Latin America through an ongoing articulation and praxis of the message and work of Jesus. In his introduction to *Christology at the Crossroads*, Sobrino clearly states the praxic dimension of his Christology: "to give Latin Americans a better understanding of Christ and to point up his historical relevancy for our continent."[15] It is not enough simply to think, speak, and write about Jesus; what is needed is the willingness to carry out his mission in a discipleship that is thoroughly committed to the liberative praxis that was modeled by the Jesus of history even unto the point of martyrdom.[16] This is the methodological position that guides liberation Christology. With this in mind, we turn now to look at the portrait of Jesus presented by Latin American liberation theologians.

13. Lois, *Christology in the Theology of Liberation*, 172.

14. Sobrino, *Christology at the Crossroads*, 305.

15. Ibid., 3.

16. In fact, Sobrino goes to the extent of speaking of martyrdom as ultimate and climactic act of faith in Jesus Christ. According to him, "surrender to Jesus in discipleship during life attains its greatest depth in surrender in death, and in that death that is properly Christian: martyrdom." Sobrino, *Jesus in Latin America*, 28.

Central Aspects of Liberation Christology

Though there are degrees of dissimilarity within liberation theologians working on Christology[17], there seems to be a marked agreement in the principal tenets they develop. The following pages briefly explore some of the common elements of Christologies of liberation.

The Historical Jesus as the Point of Departure

Whereas European quests for the historical Jesus sought mainly to establish the historical veracity of the person of Jesus, distinguishing him from the Christ of faith (the post-resurrection understanding that the early church developed concerning Jesus), the Latin American quest seeks to recover the history of Jesus by focusing on the most historical element: "his praxis and the spirit with which he carried it out."[18] Sobrino encapsulates this difference of approach in terms of the purpose each proposes to achieve. European Christologies embarked on the quest with the aim of discovering the reasonableness and meaning of the Christian faith for individuals. The quest from a Latin American perspective, however, attempts to rediscover Jesus' call to the church to do as he did—to discipleship.[19]

Liberation theologians are also not interested in distinguishing from "the *ipsissima verba Jesu* and the words of the primitive Christian

---

17. The main differences pertain to exactly how the practical/political dimensions of the Jesus of history are to be applied to the Christian setting of Latin America. Do the church and Christians need to cooperate in changing the socio-political structures that operate in Latin America? Or does the church itself need to change within the unchanged oppressive powers that resist God's kingdom? See Bussmann, *Who Do You Say?*, 48.

18. Sobrino, *Jesus the Liberator*, 51.

19. Ignacio Ellacuría beautifully summarizes this ecclesiological concern in the following manner: "The theology of liberation understands itself as a reflection from faith on the historical reality and action of the people of God, who follow the work of Jesus in announcing and fulfilling the kingdom. It understands itself as an action by the people of God in following the work of Jesus and, as Jesus did, it tries to establish a living connection between the world of God and the human world.... It is, thus, a theology that begins with historical acts and seeks to lead to historical acts, and therefore it is not satisfied with being a purely interpretive reflection; it is nourished by faithful belief in the presence of God within history, an operative presence that, although it must be grasped in grateful faith, remains an historical action." Ellacuría, "Church of the Poor," 543–64.

community," as historical Jesus studies attempt.[20] The Jesus they seek is not the "historical Jesus" but rather the "Jesus of history." They attempt to retrieve the historical facts about Jesus not in order to establish a historical foundation for Christianity, but rather to discover in the praxis of the Jesus of history the hermeneutical principle of the liberative praxis of the Christian church, thereby, establishing the paradigmatic value of the praxis of Jesus for the church today."[21]

The praxis of Jesus in this context is the whole range of activities concerning his mission and ministry, including his preaching, miracles, social (political) activity, and death. It is what he did that sheds light on who he was; and as a corollary, it is following in his steps that marks out the true believers. Liberation theologians are not interested solely in defining the correct interpretation of who Jesus was (orthodoxy), but in delineating the right manner of conduct (orthopraxis) by analyzing the practice of the Jesus of history. On this basis, they are interested not merely in theorizing about what can be known historically about Jesus of Nazareth, but in determining the ethical demands that he makes on the church. Boff defends the view of starting with the Jesus of history in this manner:

> Because the historical Jesus sheds clear light on the chief elements of Christological faith: i.e., following his life and his cause in one's own life. It is in this following that the truth of Jesus surfaces; and it is truth insofar as it enables people to transform this sinful world into the kingdom of God . . .[22]

Therefore, the Latin American search for the historical Jesus contends that knowledge of the Jesus of history is empty unless it results from analyzing his praxis. Thus, the fundamental task of liberation theologians in recreating the Jesus of history involves determining not only what the minimal structure of Jesus' practice was, but also, in popular terminology, what Jesus would do today in light of the present realities of oppression and poverty in our world.

20. Bussmann, *Who Do You Say?*, 49.

21. Depuis, *Introducción a la Cristología*, 47–48.

22. Boff, *Jesus Christ Liberator*, 279.

Jesus, the Kingdom of God, and the Poor

From this viewpoint, then, the search for the Jesus of history from a Latin American perspective begins with the recovery of the fundamental content of the praxis of Jesus: the liberation of the oppressed. The Synoptic accounts about Jesus reveal a man who was decidedly in favor of the poor, the outcast, and the oppressed (e.g., Matt 9:36; 14:14; 15:32; Mark 6:34; 8:2). What was central to the proclamation of Jesus was the dawning of the kingdom of God, and crucial to this message was the "good news" that the kingdom would bring to the marginalized people of his day (Matt 5:3; Luke 6:20). Thus, liberation theologians seek to develop their Christologies from the perspective of the periphery, for that is where the praxis of Jesus is most to be found.

That the Synoptic Gospels deal with the political dimensions of Jesus' life is not something new that theologians of liberation have discovered. What is strikingly fresh is their innovative attempt to contextualize Jesus' politics as part of the task for the church today. Thus, the liberationists' approach to "understanding Jesus, as opposed to recovering Jesus, requires holding together in creative fusion two distinct horizons: the historical Jesus of the gospels and the historical context of contemporary Latin America."[23]

Claus Bussmann classifies the four areas in which Jesus' political activities are discovered:

1. the new assessment of the prophetic element in Jesus' life and teaching

2. the new assessment of the relationship of individuals and structures

3. the new attention to Jesus' praxis

4. the new considerations of the relationship between biblical tradition and revolution.[24]

First of all, the prophetic role of Jesus is placed in the context of the Old Testament prophets. Sobrino explains Jesus' prophetic ministry in this manner:

---

23. Pope-Levison and Levison, *Jesus in Global Contexts*, 31.

24. Bussmann, *Who Do You Say?*, 51.

> Jesus' basic stance is defending the oppressed, denouncing the oppressors and unmasking the oppression that passes itself of as good and justifies itself through religion. This praxis is what makes Jesus like the prophets in his fate too: the anti-Kingdom reacts and puts him to death.[25]

Like the prophets of the Old Testament, Jesus' prophetic stance confronted the social structures of his day, demanding justice and calling for repentance. This can be seen in the content of his prophetic proclamation: the coming kingdom of God.

The fact that there are few references in the Bible outside of the Gospels concerning the in-breaking of the kingdom of God on the earth attests that it was of central importance for the preaching of Jesus of history. According to Boff:

> The fundamental project of Jesus was to proclaim and to be the instrument of the concrete realization of the absolute meaning of the world: i.e., liberation from every stigma (including suffering, division, sin, and death) and liberation for real life, for open-ended communication of love, grace and plenitude in God.[26]

Thus, at the inauguration of his ministry, Jesus programmatically outlined his principal task of proclaiming the kingdom of God in his quotation of the Isaiah text. He came "to bring good news to the poor. . .to proclaim release to the captives and recovery of sight to the blind, to let the oppressed go free, to proclaim the year of the Lord's favor" (Luke 4:18–19; cf. Isa 61:1–3).[27]

The preaching of the kingdom of God was not, therefore, simply the proclamation of a future utopia, for which the poor and oppressed of Jesus' day could long. Rather, the message of Jesus concerning the kingdom was about a reality that had irrupted within the history of humanity. The long awaited reign of God had come, and the proofs of its manifestation were the works of Jesus on behalf of the oppressed. In the words of Sobrino, "what the kingdom of God consists of can be discovered by considering Jesus' actions as actions in the service of the

25. Sobrino, *Jesus the Liberator*, 179.

26. Boff, *Jesus Christ Liberator*, 280–81.

27. In addition, it should be recognized that the prophetic utterances that reference the birth of Jesus in Luke reveal the political dimensions that the ministry of Jesus would curtail, especially in favor of the poor. See Luke 1:51–53, 69–75.

kingdom."[28] It is on the basis of Jesus' actions that the liberation of the poor and the outcast can be proclaimed as the will of God, which needs to be brought into fruition in the world.

Building on the concept of Jesus as the liberator of the poor and the oppressed, Christology takes on a different form. Instead of simply hypothesizing about what exactly happened at the incarnation, how one can understand the nature of the person of Jesus, or what theories of atonement make the most sense, liberation Christology turns to the ethical demands the historical Jesus made and continues to make.[29] Given that the historical Jesus committed his life to the service of those in need of liberation, all theologizing about his life should inevitably be aligned with the convictions he held. Through the lens of the marginalized, thus, the Jesus of history becomes the focal point in which God expresses his solidarity with the victims of every kind of injustice. In short, the understanding of the salvific work of Jesus—his life, death and resurrection—take on new meaning for those suffering all types of oppression.

The Meaning of Jesus' Death

The depiction of the Jesus of history provided by the Gospel narratives reveals the destiny of those who counteract the religious, social, and political forces that foster an environment of oppression: death. Thus, liberation theologians develop the argument that Jesus did not die; *his enemies killed him*. What led Jesus to the cross was his life of solidarity with the poor, which drove him to disturb the structures that oppressed them.[30]

Under these basic premises, the death of Jesus becomes the focus of insightful questions predicated by the view from the periphery. What does Jesus' death signify for those living in extreme conditions

---

28. Sobrino, *Jesus in Latin America*, 143.

29. This is not to say that liberation theology ignores the classical questions of Christology. On the contrary, it seeks to make the classical tenets of Christology relevant for the Latin American situation. In Sobrino's words, "liberation Christology has not explicitly set itself the task of this development, but it recognizes and acknowledges the radicalness with which the formulas of the New Testament and the councils of the first centuries profess Christ 'true God and true man.'" Sobrino, *Jesus in Latin America*, 14.

30. Sobrino, *Jesus the Liberator*, 209–10.

of poverty and oppression? What of the hope that the historical Jesus had kindled upon his hearers, did it die with him? How did his death serve to bring about the kingdom of God? Did his premature death bring an end to his program of liberation, as his enemies conspired? Was his death purposeful in terms of being the catalyst for the creation of a new society in which everyone would live out the principles of the kingdom?

Liberation Christology seeks to interpret the event of the cross as Jesus' ultimate expression of solidarity with the oppressed of the world. Thus, the hermeneutical key to understanding the death of Jesus is the identification of the *Crucified One with the crucified peoples*.[31] Having dedicated his life to the service of the poor and the oppressed, he died sharing with them the agony of their pain. What is more, on the cross, the Jesus of history reveals a suffering God who fulfills his purposes in history through weakness and love, and not retribution and force. Through the cross, God participates in the suffering of the world and it is in this act of solidarity that the crucified peoples can find a hope for the future.[32] The hope for the crucified peoples is faith in the resurrection of the Crucified One.

The Significance of the Resurrection

Liberationist reflection on the resurrection of Jesus seeks to interpret this eschatological event from the viewpoint of the crucified peoples— those whose daily life is the lived experience of dealing with the injustice and oppression of this world. It is through the lens of those whom society continues to crucify today by means of ethical and economic subjugation that liberation theologians find meaning in the resurrection of Jesus. God's act of raising the Crucified One from the dead gives birth to resurrection hope for the crucified peoples of today.

Yet, what is this hope? Is it a mere aspiration of future liberation or does the resurrection of Jesus have present liberative implications for people living in extreme conditions of impoverishment and oppression? Can the hope of the crucified of history crystallize into a reality

31. The great emphasis on this theme in the writings of Jon Sobrino has prompted the title to one of the most recent studies in his Christology. Stålsett, *Crucified and the Crucified*.

32. Ibid., 244–45.

that manifests itself in the present, enabling them to experience life rather than death? For liberation theologians, the answer to this last question is a definite yes.

Such a hope can become a reality because the Risen One is the Crucified One; the one who died in the hands of an unjust society is the one who was raised by the just God, who in doing so defeats the evils of injustice. Sobrino affirms:

> Jesus' resurrection is not only a symbol of God's omnipotence, then–as if God had decided arbitrarily and without any connection with Jesus' life and lot to show how powerful he was. Rather, Jesus' resurrection is presented as God's response to the unjust, criminal action of human beings. Hence God's action in response is understood in conjunction with the human activity that provokes this response: the murder of the Just One. Pictured in this way, the resurrection of Jesus shows *in directo* the triumph of justice over injustice.[33]

Through the resurrection, the victims of injustice receive a credible hope of being themselves resurrected and living as risen ones. The good news that the resurrection of Jesus manifests is that "once and for all justice has triumphed over injustice."[34]

Jesus in the *Barrio*: Christological Reflections from the Margins

Having looked at the ideology, methodology, and the central aspects of liberation Christology, we now turn to analyze the foundational elements of Christology from a Hispanic perspective.[35] Though there have

---

33. Sobrino, *Jesus in Latin America*, 149.

34. Ibid.

35. It should be noted that there are many differences between the reality lived by Latin Americans and that of Hispanics living in the U.S. Though, we share a common ancestry, having our ethnic roots firmly planted in Latin America, our experience in the U.S. is necessarily different from that of those who live in Latin America. Thus, a Hispanic Christology will seek to be relevant to the realities and experiences of the various Hispanic communities living in the U.S. For a more in-depth conversation concerning the differences between Latin Americans and Hispanics and their significance for theological reflection, consult De La Torre, *Introducing Latino/a Theologies*, 9–40.

been various studies in Hispanic Christology, there is still much work to be done.[36]

Before we proceed, however, some clarification is needed. Though there can be no question as to the importance that liberation Christology has in the development of a contextual Latino/a Christology, some dangers must be pointed out. The foundational element of liberation Christology does not compel a slavish reproduction of christological themes in the guise of Hispanic ideologies.[37] The quest is not merely for a "plug and play" application where parallel substitution suffices. Rather, in the process of development, the same critiques launched at liberation Christology will need to be taken into consideration, resulting in a more solid foundation.

What is more, the reader has certainly been left with many questions concerning the adequacy of liberation Christology and the foundation it may serve for Hispanic Christologies. Many hermeneutical issues were passed over without proper investigation to establish its legitimacy and underscore its inadequacies, simply to highlight the value of liberation Christology. However, for a thorough presentation of Christology from a Hispanic perspective (which is not the aim of this chapter) a solid argumentation of its methodological approach would be needed in order to establish its contextual aims. What is presented in the following pages, then, are the characteristic features and main themes developed thus far in Hispanic approaches to Christology.

Jesus el Mestizo: Ethnicity/Race and Christological Discourse

A key issue in beginning to think theologically about Jesus Christ from a Hispanic perspective is the need for Hispanic Christology to be relevant to the living conditions of Hispanics living in the U.S. The goal for a Hispanic Christology, then, is to be a contextual reflection on the

36. Here I refer mainly to the seminal works of Orlando E. Costas (*Christ outside the Gate*), Virgilio Elizondo (*Galilean Journey*), and Roberto S. Goizueta (*Caminemos con Jesus*), and the emerging voices of which Luis G. Pedraja (*Jesus Is My Uncle*) is an example, which have and continue to develop christological reflections from a Hispanic perspective.

37. In fact, one of the major criticisms that have been launched at early attempts at Hispanic Christology has been that they merely imitate liberation Christologies with a thin Hispanic veneer. Thus, as with liberation theology at its inception, Hispanic/Latino theology has been asked to produce a truly authentic Hispanic Christology.

life and work of Jesus. Stephen B. Bevans defines contextual theology like this:

> Contextual theology can be defined as a way of doing theology in which one takes into account: the spirit and message of the gospel; the tradition of the Christian people; the culture in which one is theologizing; and the social change in that culture, whether brought about by western technological process or the grass-roots struggle for equality, justice and liberation.[38]

Following these principles of contextualization, we need to understand properly the place from which Hispanic theology arises. What is the Latino reality that Hispanic Christology seeks to address? What is the social location from which its theological inquiry departs?

First, we attach special significance to the distinctive characteristics of the Jesus of history that parallel our condition as Hispanics, mainly that of living in a state of marginality. In *Galilean Journey*, Virgilio Elizondo compares the Mexican-American struggle against marginalization, oppression, and discrimination with the life of Jesus the Galilean. Concerning Jesus' experience with marginalization, he says:

> As a Galilean, Jesus grew up in contact with diverse peoples and cultures, yet far from all the "centers of belongings"—political, intellectual, or religious. Rejected and put down by all the in-groups of their world, the Galileans had learned through their margination and suffering to relativize society's absolutes.[39]

Relating Jesus' struggle with that of Hispanics living in the U.S., he writes in another book:

> In the midst of this confusion, an experience of good news suddenly began among the poor and destitute of society. One of the marginated ones now became the source of solidarity and messianic hope among the masses of hopeless people. He was no well-intentioned outsider or missioner. Out of the ranks of the nobodies of the world, own of their own became the source of friendship, community and hope. This is the core of the *evangelium*.[40]

---

38. Bevans, *Models of Contextual Theology*, 1.

39. Elizondo, *Galilean Journey*, 55.

40. Elizondo, *Future Is Mestizo*, 74.

There is also an incarnational dimension to Hispanic Christology. Jesus became a man, but a man whose incarnation took place among a specific people, and in a particular time and place. The life of the Jesus of history is seen as that of an alien in his own land: born in the land of his ancestors, but under the control of a foreign power, which sought to suppress their cultural distinctiveness. The entire rights and privileges of a "citizen" were not available to him despite living in his own land; he was a foreigner in his own land. In many ways, this parallels the life of many Hispanics living in the U.S., where minorities continue to be marginalized by the dominant culture. Beginning with this viewpoint, what is the christological picture that the Gospels and the rest of the New Testament portray? What does the kingdom of God promise? How does the death and resurrection of Jesus translate into good news for those living in a state of marginalization?

It is in the life of Jesus that God comes to inhabit our world and seeks to transform it from within. According to Orlando E. Costas, "the incarnation forces us to contextualize God's activity within history, preventing us from turning God into an abstract being removed from human experience."[41] The cross is the place where God judges and condemns every sort of alienation. Moreover, the resurrection not only points to the future complete transformation of humanity into the multicultural people of God, but proleptically announces it in the dawning of a new community: the church.

Christ outside the Gate: Poverty and Marginality as Locus Theologicus

Another dimension of Hispanic Christology is its missional approach. Jesus' mission during his earthly ministry is summarized in Luke 4:16: "he came to set the captives free!" It was a mission to the poor and dispossessed of the world, to those hurting and those in need because of the injustices of the reigning world order. Thus, instead of seeking to understand the person of Jesus through philosophical arguments regarding his nature, what becomes more significant is what Jesus did; for we can only truly understand who someone is by what they do. Thus, Hispanic Christology focuses on following Jesus in a discipleship that imitates his prophetic mission—it is a Christology of transformation.

41. Costas, *Christ outside the Gate*, 8.

Roberto S. Goizueta calls this "a theology of accompaniment," for Jesus calls his disciples to walk with him and not follow behind him. For Goizueta this entails "an identification not only with the social-historical situation of the poor but also with [the] liberating God, the God of the poor": walking with the poor and walking with the God who became poor![42] Very much in line with liberation Christology, the focus is on reflection oriented by praxis, which again leads to praxis. For Hispanic theologians, it is not enough to simply talk about Jesus' identification with the poor, the church must follow in the ways of her Lord in serving the community and in the quest to establish peace and justice for all.

Goizueta concretely establishes the point of departure for Hispanic theology in Christocentric fashion.

> [T]he *locus* of theology is the *physical, spatial* and *geographical place* of theological reflection. To walk with Jesus and with the poor is to walk *where* Jesus walks and *where* the poor walked. . . . In a society where barriers, spatial separation, isolation, and distance are chief means of exclusion and oppression, a theology from the perspective of the poor cannot ignore the importance of physical, location, or space, as a theological category.[43]

In metaphorical sense, then, both Costas and Goizueta call for a christocentric theology that desires to walk with Jesus outside the gates of the church in accompaniment of the people whom the church seeks to serve.

Jesus Is My Uncle: A Relational/Incarnational Christology

Another distinguishing mark of Hispanic Christology is its relational and incarnational aspect. For example, after establishing the importance of the incarnation of Christ for Hispanics, Luis G. Pedraja explores the dimension of discipleship in a chapter entitled "God Is a Verb." In order to comprehend the nuance that Pedraja is making by using this title, it is important to understand what he calls "reading the Bible in Spanish," which leads to "doing Christology in Spanish."[44] The Spanish translation

42. Goizueta, *Caminemos con Jesús*, 211.

43. Ibid., 191–92.

44. Pedraja, *Jesus Is My Uncle*, 85–89. See also, Pedraja, "Doing Christology in Spanish," 462–63.

of the Greek word *logos* in John 1:1 is "verbo" (verb), as opposed to "word" in English. The main difference this makes in reading the text is that whereas "word" has a static connotation, "verb" has dynamic implications. Thus, even in the name of the eternal *logos*, the actions of the "Verb" (his praxis) are seen as significant for doing Christology not just as an academic exercise but also in our imitation of his praxis. Pedraja puts it this way:

> God's revelation is not just a set of concepts, but a way of living. It is not just information; it is also action. It is not just *what* is revealed that matters, but also *how* it is revealed. Jesus' actions and our understanding of his relationship to God have serious implications for our own lives. Furthermore, Jesus' life and actions indicate how we should understand God's relationship with humanity and how God is present in humanity.
>
> As Christians, we believe not only that God acted in the life of Jesus of Nazareth but also that God still acts in our lives as well. It is through these actions, exemplified concretely in the flesh through Jesus' love and through God's incarnate presence in him, that we ultimately encounter God's presence in history and in humanity—a presence that is not limited to the historical person of Jesus of Nazareth.[45]

Thus, Hispanic Christology calls for following Jesus' praxis of love and justice. Far from simply seeking to articulate a philosophical understanding of the nature and person of Christ, its goal is to embody Jesus' praxis of love and justice as a principle for discipleship, to denounce the injustices of this world and announce the justice of the reign of God, all of which result from a prophetic approach to doing theology.

Jesus, Prophet of Social Change

Jorge A. Aquino highlights the prophetic christological dimensions of Latina/o theology in this way:

> [T]he Scriptures present an image of Jesus as a humble man, not a wealthy, well-to-do person. A reading of the fiery sermons he gave in Jerusalem in the days before his crucifixion indicates that he was persecuted because he tried to bring his poor-people's Good News to the Jerusalem establishment (during the holiest season of the Jewish year, no less: the Passover). His real

45. Pedraja, *Jesus Is My Uncle*, 88.

transgression was to bring before the powers of his time an attitude of protest against the prevailing structures of oppression and hypocrisy in his society. The "wrong place" that Jesus walked with his impoverished and outcast followers was not so much the geographical ghetto of poverty and marginality—in his case, Galilee and its environs—but Jerusalem: the capital of a Jewish world under Roman occupation. He brought his rabble before the powers and got into a lot of hot water. Jesus was a prophet, and a daring and angry one at that, judging from the situations of his discourses and his high-and-mighty audiences.[46]

The significant—and indeed much needed—critique that Aquino develops is the directionality of prophetic witness. Latina/o Christology does not merely point to the poor and marginalized and say, "Look, we need to fix that." Instead it is a prophetic discourse from within the position of the poor and marginalized of society. Alluding to the title of a book by Harold J. Recinos, one might say that the good news is not simply taken *to* the *barrio*, but it is where it comes *from*.[47] The Son of God incarnate became a man within a marginalized people; he experienced life as one who is poor. In that condition, he spoke out to the religious and political authorities of his day denouncing their injustices and announcing the justice of the God's reign. Latina/o Christology focuses on what it means today to live as Jesus did: to follow him and his actions.

Latina Perspectives on Jesus

A more recent and much needed contribution to the construction of Hispanic Christology is the insight from Latina theologians. Alicia Vargas explains the need for elaborating a Latina theology in general and a Latina Christology in particular:

> In addition to the profoundly ambiguous identity and social location that Latinas share with Latino men in the U.S., Latina women suffer the socio-economic and sexist oppression and discrimination that render them doubly marginal in the country where we live and have our being. . . . Plentiful are the statistical studies of results of sexism and its Spanish equivalent,

---

46. Aquino, "Prophetic Horizon of Latino Theology," 121–22.

47. Recinos, *Good News from the Barrio.*

machismo, which adds its particular sting to the life of the Latina population.[48]

In accordance to her own *mujerista* methodology, Ada María Isasi-Díaz seeks to "listen carefully to the voices of grassroots Latinas knowing that they are admirably capable of reflecting on what they believe and of explaining it in ways that contribute to liberation—fullness of life."[49] Isasi-Díaz makes three key contributions to Latina/o Christology in her development of *mujerista* Christology. The first is a reunderstanding of the "kin-dom" of God as "la Familia de Dios." Here the focus on Jesus shifts metaphors from powerful king to compassionate and suffering brother, which is in invitation for all to be sisters, brothers, sons, daughters, mothers, and fathers in imitation of Jesus. Second, Isasi-Díaz draws out the implications of Jesus who is the faithful companion of those who suffer in this world. Just as Jesus lived in true companionship to those most in need, discipleship signifies that we too live with the same kind of love and compassion toward others. Third, Isasi-Diaz unpacks the implied christological insight in the "old custom of melding 'Jesus' and 'Christ' into one word: *Jesucristo*."[50] The significance in this is that Jesus Christ implies a duality of human and divine natures, whereas *Jesucristo* emphasizes the personal relationship with the divine who walks and talks with us on a daily basis.

For Isasi-Díaz the prospect of doing Christology from a *mujerista* perspective has more to do with *living our Christology* as opposed to merely *thinking it*. This is very much at the core of Latin American and Hispanic approaches to Christology, and should also be a task of Hispanic Pentecostal Christology. Yet, while the focus of this chapter has been to establish the contextual and liberative approach of Latin American and Latina/o, before moving on to the next chapter, it is important to solidify the prospect of the contextual presentation of Jesus' life and meaning that was just presented by including a discussion of the socio-economic situation of Jesus' day. I do this over against the view that liberation and Latina/o theologies do not have an exegetical warrant to propose a Christology in terms of social analysis and the plight of the poor, and that their beliefs are merely the view of Marxist ideals.

---

48. Vargas, "Construction of a Latina Christology, 272.

49. Isasi-Díaz, "Christ in *Mujerista* Christology, 159.

50. Ibid.

Thus, I purposely refrain from leaning on Latin American and Hispanic theologians, and opt for an analysis from the perspective of contemporary New Testament studies, which uses the tools of socio-scientific analysis. I take my queue for evaluating a key theme in Hispanic theology, Jesus' identity as a poor Galilean, from Michelle A. González, who argues that a more critical analysis of Latina/o Christology in light of New Testament scholarship is needed.[51]

Excursus: Jesus and the Socio-Economic Situation of His Day

The Socio-Economic Situation of the Mediterranean World

Jesus' concern for the poor is a significant theme in the Gospel of Luke. This can be seen in Jesus' programmatic opening proclamation ("The Spirit of the Lord is upon me, because he has anointed me to bring good news to the poor"; 4:18); in his teaching to the disciples ("Blessed are you who are poor, for yours is the kingdom of God"; 6:20); and in his message to John the Baptist (". . .the poor have good news brought to them"; 7:22). The poor also appear prominently in his table conversations with the affluent, his parables, his meetings with the rich, and in Jesus' observation at the temple treasury.

An assessment of Jesus' attitude toward the poor, however, requires a careful examination of the socio-economic situation of Palestine where he lived and ministered. Establishing the economic situation of Jesus' day allows for a proper grounding of his words and actions on account of the poor. Moreover, because Jesus has much to say about property and riches, his attitude toward the wealthy must also be taken into account. How does the socio-economic context of Palestine serve to nuance Jesus' words and actions concerning the poor? How does Jesus' attitude toward the rich serve as a contrast to his attitude toward the poor?

In order to understand the socio-economic situation of Jesus' day, we will follow the guidelines and principles set forth by Ekkehard W. Stegemann and Wolfgang Stegemann in their book *The Jesus Movement*.

---

51. González, "Jesus," 22.

Thus, this section outlines the results of their social-scientific approach to Jesus and his times, with special consideration of how their findings nuance Jesus' actions, words, and attitudes.

Stegemann and Stegemann classify the type of society that existed in the ancient Mediterranean world as an *advanced agrarian society*. The term "agrarian" expresses the idea that "the economic backbone of these states was agriculture" and that "the overwhelming majority of the population lived in the country and by agriculture."[52] However, in describing Mediterranean societies as agrarian one should not overlook the social structures that controlled the rural population and its production. "[T]he economic importance of cities, especially in the areas of skilled labor and trade, and as the consumers of agricultural production," reveals another facet of Mediterranean agrarian societies: the elite who lived in the city owned the land and wealth, which provided them with power both in the city and in the country.[53] Thus, agricultural production was regulated and redistributed by the ruling classes, which resulted in a society where wealth belonged to a small number of the elite. The reason that Mediterranean agrarian societies are further labeled as "advanced" is due first to their technological advances, but even more to the Roman Empire because of the relative advance in the type of economic system and the social conditions it created. What we are talking about here, then, is neither a horticultural society nor an industrial one, but rather a posthorticultural yet preindustrial society: an advanced agrarian society.[54]

Based on this brief presentation of the characteristics of ancient Mediterranean economy, it can be said that two of the most important factors were agriculture (that is, the production of foods) and the burdening of the population by the elite that resulted from the redistribution of goods and services. As a result of this sort of economic system, the living conditions of the landowning elite differed widely from that of the non-landowners.

Since land ownership was the principal means for obtaining and increasing wealth, the elite always sought to possess more and more land. (The largest landowners, of course, were the emperors themselves,

52. Stegemann and Stegemann, *Jesus Movement*, 7.

53. Ibid.

54. Ibid., 10.

followed by various subdivisions of the elite.) Creating a surplus and making a profit were possibilities that only those who owned land could realistically accomplish. However, the land that was owned needed cultivation, and this was carried out by tenant farmers, day laborers, and slaves. The land was leased to farmers in exchange for either rent or a share of the harvest. Aside from any contractual stipulations, either written or verbal, that may have existed, it is known through primary sources that oftentimes "subtenants were exploited by the main lease-holders and not only had to pay their rents but also had to make their labor available beyond the period agreed upon."[55] Moreover, crop failures due to droughts or other natural catastrophes did not serve to free the tenant farmer from the agreed upon contract. The consequences of dealing first with paying the rent or giving up the share of the harvest to the landowner meant that the farmers and their families many times starved. To complicate further the living conditions of these tenant farmers, one has to keep in mind that many times the landowners "graciously" allowed the farmers to become indebted to them, and that the farmers also had to pay levies and taxes on the land and its yield.

The great machinery that was the Roman Empire operated on a system of compulsory levies, forced labor, and excessive taxes. Every province of the empire had to contribute to the Roman state. Two basic expenditures that compulsory agricultural levies paid for was the provisioning of the Roman military and the population of Rome. Stegemann and Stegemann calculate the amount of grain needed to feed the Roman military for a year at 100,000 tons of grain. "This amount of grain would correspond to an approximate need of 375,000 to 500,000 acres of land,"[56] meaning an area three to four times the size of Galilee's arable land (125,000 acres) would have been needed. In addition to this, the provisioning of the one million inhabitants of Rome would require twice the amount needed for the troops; that is, about 1,500,000 acres of agricultural land. Opportunely, at the time the Roman Empire had at its disposal hundreds of conquered territories similar to Galilee, which they could burden by extorting high taxes in order to feed the Roman legions and the Roman population.

55. Stegemann and Stegemann here refer to an inscription found in the *Corpus inscriptionum latinarum* 8.10570 and 14464 that describes the condition in one imperial domain in Africa. Ibid., 46.

56. Ibid., 47.

Furthermore, in order to construct and maintain public works (roads, wastewater disposal, bridges, aqueducts, etc.) throughout its domain, the Roman Empire relied on forced labor that many times was funded by the resident population, except mainly in Italy. But what burdened the poor rural population the most was the excessive taxes that existed throughout the Mediterranean world, which meant that "the vast majority of the rural populace in antiquity lived on the fine line between hunger and assurance of subsistence."[57] This phenomenon could be more clearly appreciated in Stegemann and Stegemann's stratification of ancient Mediterranean societies.

The main criteria of stratification that Stegemann and Stegemann use are power, privilege, and prestige, which determine a society's system of distribution. "[These] are the most important variables in determining the social position of a person in the social system."[58] Following their carefully thought out and explained criteria, they offer a heuristic model for determining the social position of a person in the societies of the Roman empire.[59] The model divides ancient societies into two basic groups, the elite (upper stratum) and the non-elite (lower stratum).[60]

---

57. Ibid., 51.

58. Here Stegemann and Stegemann follow Gerhard Lenski, who views *power* as the primary variable because it "determines how a society's surplus [the excess of production over need] will be divided." Moreover, *privileges* are dependant on power, since they reveal the "possession or control of a part of the surplus that a society produces." Lastly, Lenski considers *prestige* as being a function of both power and privilege. Lenski, *Power and Privilege*; quoted in Stegemann and Stegemann, *Jesus Movement*, 61.

59. A skeleton model is presented in Stegemann and Stegemann, *Jesus Movement*, 68–71, followed later by a more elaborate presentation on 71–95.

60. Stegemann and Stegemann are not alone in ruling out the existence of a middle class in ancient Mediterranean societies. Lenski's study, for example, categorizes nine classes, five upper and four lower, separated by an abysmal gulf. However, some scholars attempt to find a middle class. For example, Karl Christ gathers various social groups (free farmers on their own land, urban freed slaves with small workshops, free artisans in general, and merchants). Stegemann and Stegemann perceive this as a failed attempt at establishing the existence of a middle class because "even the ancient authors themselves reveal no awareness of a middle stratum whose status rests between the upper and the lower strata." *Jesus Movement*, 68. As convincing as their position is, due to the painstaking monetary breakdown that explains what belonging to the upper and lower classes meant, their study could have been strengthened by a more elaborate description of what it would have meant to belong to a middle class. If a middle class had existed, how much power, privilege, and prestige would one have needed to belong to it?

The upper stratum was made up of three main populations: (a) the members of the Roman *ordines* (which included the imperial aristocracy [*domus Caesaris*], senatorial nobility [*ordo senatorius*], and equestrians [*ordo equester*]) and the ruling houses and priestly families in vassal states and provinces; (b) rich people who did not possess political titles or offices; and (c) retainers, that is, "the free individuals, freed slaves, and slaves who assumed duties for their masters in prominent political positions or performed important administrative tasks in the private sphere."[61] Lenski calculates the governing class at 1–2 percent of the population and the retainer class at 5 percent, thus, even with conservative estimates at most the upper stratum of the population consisted of about 10 percent. Considering that the estimated total population of the Roman Empire in the third century was 70 million, there is quite a substantial difference of population when compared to the lower stratum.

In order to subdivide the lower stratum, Stegemann and Stegemann differentiate between the relatively poor (or the relatively prosperous) and the absolutely poor. The dividing line between these groupings is the calculated sum of what it would take to live at a level of minimum existence. Those above the line of minimum existence are considered relatively poor, and those below the line as absolutely poor. It is appropriate to point out here that although a sizeable percentage could live at minimum existence, their lack of power and the vast disparity in the acquisition of wealth, land ownership, and continued indebtedness in comparison to that of the upper stratum does not allow for the designation "middle class."

After calculating that the food necessary for an adult to survive for "one year would require the expenditure of almost 70 denarii," Stegemann and Stegemann estimate that the minimum yearly income for a family of four living in the country (including additional costs for clothing and taxes) to remain at minimum existence would be about 250 to 300 denarii.[62] In comparison, the cost of living in the city would require about two times that amount (600 to 700), and three times the amount (900 to 100 denarii) if the city was Rome. Since the annual salary of a day laborer amounted to about 200 denarii, the continual hand-to-mouth existence of these people would clearly prevent them

---

61. Ibid., 69.
62. Ibid., 83.

from even a minimal degree of monetary accumulation and almost completely rule out the possibility of acquiring a small piece of land.

The terminology ancient authors used also helps us to distinguish between the relatively poor and the absolutely poor. Both πτωχὸς and πένης can signify "poor," but a more specific sense for each is given in the following text. Aristophanes writes, "the nature of the life of the πτωχὸς is to have nothing. That of the πένης, however, is to be frugal and devote himself to work; he has nothing left over, but he also suffers no need."[63] Thus, Stegemann and Stegemann provide a definition for each: "πτωχὸς usually means the poor who live on the verge or even below minimum existence, whereas πένης describes an economic situation in which someone can earn a living for himself and his family through work."[64] The absolutely poor, then, are those who lack the most basic of human needs of food, clothing, and shelter.

The Socio-Economic Situation of New Testament Palestine

Having outlined the socio-economic situation in the ancient Mediterranean world, we turn now to consider the situation in Palestine at the time of Jesus. As any other province of the time, Palestine was under Roman control. Due to the great extent of arable land, Palestine was not just another colony; its vast agricultural space made it a very desirable land.[65] The control of the land in Palestine, therefore, was a determining factor as to who had power, prestige, and privilege.

The population of first-century Palestine could be divided into two major groups of people: the rich and the poor.[66] The elite or upper stratum included the Herodian family, the remnants of the older Jewish aristocracy, the high-priestly clans, and prosperous merchants. Presumably, Herod considered all of Palestine as his property, but it is estimated that the Herodian family did indeed come to own more than half of the land.[67] In addition to this, the high taxes imposed upon the

63. Aristophanes *Plutos* 11.328.

64. Stegemann and Stegemann, *Jesus Movement*, 89.

65. Concerning Galilee's agriculture Josephus says, "it is entirely under cultivation and produces crops from one end to the other..." Josephus *J.W.* 3.4.

66. For a brief account, see Davids, "Rich and Poor," 701–10. For a more extensive treatment, see Hanson and Oakman, *Palestine in the Time of Jesus*, 63–129; and also Stegemann and Stegemann, *Jesus Movement*, 104–36.

67. Davids, "Rich and Poor," 702.

masses brought great wealth to the Herodians. In order to collect the obligatory tribute that Palestine had to pay Rome, the Jewish aristocracy, along with the highest bidding tax leaseholders, would compete for the right to taxation and in turn receive the aid of the needed Roman military force. Such power of taxation resulted in great privilege and prestige of the upper stratum over against the lower stratum.

The second major category of people in first-century Palestine was the poor or lower stratum. Anyone outside the circle of power that belonged to the ruling elite would be part of this category. Among them were those who somehow managed to live at minimum existence (small landowners, tenant farmers, artisans, small traders, fishermen, hired laborers, indebted servants and slaves), and those who lived below that level (beggars, prostitutes, shepherds, and bandits). The characteristics most descriptive of this group of people were their continual exploitation by the rich, their incapacity to create a surplus, and their almost complete lack of land. Percentage wise, the great majority of the population of Palestine was poor in comparison to the small minority of the upper stratum.

The privileged condition of the upper stratum had devastating results on the rest of the population. Three major problems resulted from these circumstances. The majority of the land was owned by a few, resulting in a lack of land—"a shortage of agriculturally usable land per capita of population, [where] more and more people had to earn their living from less and less land."[68] As stated before, the acquisition of large portions of land led to the rental of such lands to tenant farmers who would work the land. Land ownership was the key determinant of a person's wealth. This system resulted in the abuse of hired tenants and laborers.

A second problem was high taxation. P. H. Davids calculates the combined Roman and religious taxes to be paid per person at 17–23 percent of a person's gross income.[69] Remembering that the majority of the people barely earned enough to survive, when one takes into account the size of a person's family, which meant not only an added cost of living expenses but also higher taxes, the taxes imposed on them were catastrophic.

68. Stegemann and Stegemann, *Jesus Movement*, 112.
69. Davids, "Rich and Poor," 703.

The third problem was that of increased indebtedness. In general, the client-patron relationship that existed in the first-century world resulted in a favorable alliance between the Roman aristocracy and its vassal ruling families.[70] This upper tier of clients and patrons was in a better bargaining position than lower-tier clients and patrons. The elite patrons (e.g., the emperors) who tended over their elite clients (e.g., the Herodian family) procured their own honor, status, and power. These elite clients, in turn, established relationships of patronage with those under them. The predicament that resulted from this situation was a state of social inequality and dependency. Put in simple terms, the system favored those who, though clients themselves, could be in a relationship of patronage toward others. These others, however, always remained clients. Richard A. Horsley further describes the problem of indebtedness as follows:

> It is the means by which the dynamics of the Roman imperial situation in Palestine resulted in other forms of social malaise. Despair as well as poverty and hunger plagued the pressured peasantry generally, but particularly those who had lost their traditional lands or whose situation was deteriorating. As some families lost their land to, or came under the power of, the wealthy and powerful creditors, village communities disintegrated.[71]

A very vivid description of the problem of indebtedness is found in the parable of the unjust steward (Luke 16:1–9). This parable illustrates the ladder of indebtedness between patrons and clients; the lower one is on the ladder, the more one is indebted. That the parable deals with the problem of extreme indebtedness very accurately reflects the overall situation in first-century Palestine.

---

70. A description of what the patronage system entailed would be useful here. "Patrons are elite persons (male or female) who can provide benefits to others on a personal basis, due to a combination of superior power, influence, reputation, position, and wealth. In return for these benefits, patrons... could expect to receive honor, information, and political support from clients. Clients, on the other hand, are persons of lesser status who are obligated and loyal to a patron over a period of time. In Roman society patronage/clientage was a clearly defined relationship between individuals of different status for their mutual benefit." Hanson and Oakman, *Palestine in the Time of Jesus*, 70–71.

71. Horsley, *Sociology and the Jesus Movement*, 89–90.

It is not surprising that the three main problems briefly described here resulted in the increased social unrest of the Palestinian populace. As a consequence of the lack of land, the heavy burden of taxation, and extreme indebtedness, the lower stratum of Palestinian society became powerless and fell victim to the upper stratum. Since politics, religion, and economics went hand in hand, the upper stratum (the ruling and priestly families) had control over the land and its production. In response to this exploitation, various revolutionary groups arose in resistance to the injustices brought on by the socio-economic system. One only needs to point to the fact that the revolutionary movements burnt debt records as an act of solidarity with the indebted masses.[72] By burning the records of their debt, they sought to rally the poor to join the fight against the upper stratum of society that continued to impoverish them.

When one considers that Jesus met the same fate as the many social bandits and revolutionary leaders of his day, one has to consider if there is at least a contextual link between them. Although one might not place Jesus in the same category as Judas the Galilean, one has to admit that in many ways the same socio-economic context affected their way of thinking, their vision of what Palestine should be, and the actions that resulted from their convictions.

Jesus and the Good News to the Poor

In light of the socio-economic and political context that existed in Jesus' day, it is important to frame his life and family within it. Answering basic questions concerning the economic status of his family serve to help understand the world that shaped Jesus' thought and actions. Given the social unrest that existed in Galilee throughout his life, it is important to consider how that social situation might have affected him and his family. Only then can we begin to answer the question as to how those circumstances gave form to his proclamation of the kingdom of God. Did Jesus preach and teach without concern for the situation that his people were experiencing? Were his words detached from the lived reality of occupied Roman Palestine? Was his message of mere spiritual content or did it have a socio-economic and political edge to it?

---

72. Josephus *J. W.* 2.427. In fact, peasant indebtedness was one of the major motives behind the Jewish revolt. See Goodman, "First Jewish Revolt," 418–27.

Though it would require much more space to adequately develop Jesus' socio-economic situation, a few well-established historical facts concerning his family upbringing will suffice to place Jesus within the lower stratum of first-century Palestine. First, Jesus' birth narrative reveals some specific information with regard to his social status. Jesus was born in a small town in Galilee called Nazareth to a young peasant virgin named Mary. That Mary had a peasant upbringing is evidenced in her song of praise after her meeting with Elizabeth: "He has brought down the powerful from their thrones, and lifted up the lowly; he has filled the hungry with good things, and sent the rich away empty" (Luke 1:52–53). The type of sacrifice offered at the time of Jesus' presentation in the temple reveals that their economic situation prevented them from bringing the required lamb for a burnt offering and a pigeon or turtledove for a sin offering. Instead, in accordance with the Levitical guidelines for those who could not afford it (Lev 12:8), they brought "a pair of turtledoves or two young pigeons" (Luke 2:23–24). These two facts speak of the economic situation into which Jesus was born.

Second, Jesus' earthly father's profession of a carpenter (τέκτων) informs us of the economic situation during his early life (Matt 13:55). Although the exact occupation of a τέκτων can be debated (a carpenter, a mason, one who makes plows or yokes, or maybe a jack-of-all-trades construction worker), one thing is certain: his family belonged to the lower stratum.

According to Stegemann and Stegemann, as a carpenter Joseph would hardly have earned more than a day laborer; at best, his annual income could have been about 400 denarii.[73] Now remembering their conclusions regarding minimum existence (that family of four would require 250–300 denarii per year to subsist), Joseph's income would barely be above it. When one considers the size of Jesus' family, an even tighter budget needs to be imagined. They numbered at least nine (mother, father, five sons, and at least two daughters; Mark 6:3). After the sons grew up and could contribute to the family's economy, perhaps things would have been different; but while Jesus was a child, the oldest of many, things would have been very tight. Moreover, given the lack of reference to Joseph after the incident at the temple when Jesus was twelve and up to Jesus' death, one can assume that Joseph's death would

---

73. Stegemann and Stegemann, *Jesus Movement*, 90.

have brought even more financial burden to a family living at the edge of minimal existence. As the son of a widow with at least six siblings, Jesus would have tasted poverty firsthand and felt the burden that the elite of his society placed on the poor.

Third, after his father's death, Jesus continued in his steps, earning a living through the profession his father taught him. In Mark 6:3, Jesus is called "the carpenter." As the eldest son, he would be responsible for the welfare of his family. Whatever wealth or status Jesus might have gained from his profession, it certainly was not enough to acquire property as can be inferred from the gospel accounts. Jesus had no place to lay his head during the years of his wandering ministry (Matt 8:20) and was probably even buried in a borrowed tomb (Joseph of Arimathea's). Another telling incident during the ministry of Jesus speaks to his and his disciples' poverty. After seeing Jesus' disciples plucking heads of grain on the Sabbath (Mark 2:23–25), the Pharisees demand to know why he allows them to do this on this day. Jesus' response alludes to their hunger and their lack of food (v 25).

Given the socio-economic context of Palestine, what is the force of the Jesus' words regarding riches and property? What does Jesus have to say about the rich and their riches? How does this serve to contrast Jesus' attitude toward the poor? In light of the social realities of his day, in which the accumulation of riches was connected in some way with dishonest practices, Jesus' advises the rich to rethink their status in society. In other parables and conversations with regard to the rich, Jesus' stance toward the right use of riches is highlighted. In the parable of the rich fool (Luke 12:16–21), Jesus speaks of the foolishness of storing up riches that will never be used. To the rich ruler Jesus commands "sell all that you own and distribute the money to the poor, and you will have treasure in heaven; then come, follow me" (Luke 18:22). Moreover, Zacchaeus (a tax collector who made great profits at the expense of others) is set as an example of one who gives half of his possessions to the poor and promises to repay fourfold anyone he has defrauded.

Jesus' attitude toward the rich also contains a marked prophetic stance that condemns their abuses. "[W]oe to you who are rich, for you have received your consolation" (Luke 6:24). In the parable of the rich man and Lazarus (Luke 16:19–31), the rich man (who feasted sumptuously and seemingly passed by a poor man daily without giving alms) finds himself in hell tormented apparently for not making good use of his riches. Again, as an object lesson from his conversation with the rich ruler Jesus remarks: "Indeed, it is easier for a camel to go through the eye of a needle than for someone who is rich to enter the kingdom of God" (Luke 18:25).

Compared to this brief summary of socio-economic conditions and Jesus' attitude toward the rich, his attitude toward the poor in Luke stands in sharp contrast.[74] Luke's interest in the poor begins with the inclusion of Mary's song of praise. The song serves to set up the contrast that will reappear in the account of Jesus' ministry: "He has brought down the powerful from their thrones, and lifted up the lowly; he has filled the hungry with good things, and sent the rich away empty" (Luke 1:52–53). Clearly, the expectations of those who suffer because of the socio-economic and political situation will become a significant aspect of the ministry Jesus.

Jesus' inaugural proclamation in Luke ("The Spirit of the Lord is upon me, because he has anointed me to bring good news to the poor"; 4:18) presents his mission in terms of the social ramifications of his ministry. When John the Baptist sent word to inquire if he was the one who was to come (7:19), Jesus responds by sending him the signs of his messianic mission: "the blind receive their sight, the lame walk, the lepers are cleansed, the deaf hear, the dead are raised, the poor have good news brought to them" (7:22).

The good news consists in that, contrary to the social reality the poor were experiencing, the kingdom of God was theirs. "Blessed are you who are poor, for yours is the kingdom of God" (6:20). Although one could argue that in the Matthean beatitude regarding the "poor in spirit" refers metaphorically to the pious, in the Lukan version it is improbable. In a world were the kingdom belonged to the rich and the powerful, Jesus proclaimed the coming kingdom as belonging to the poor and the weak (see 18:16: "Let the little children come to me, and do not stop them; for it is to such as these that the kingdom of God belongs").

The kingdom of God appears prominently as the major theme of Jesus' proclamation (4:43; 8:1; 9:11—these verses serve to summarize the main content of his preaching). Moreover, Luke's account of the life of Jesus contains bookend comments on the expectations of the coming

74. For studies focused on Jesus and the poor, see Seccombe, *Possessions and the Poor*; and Roth, *The Blind, the Lame, and the Poor*.

kingdom (see 2:25, 38; 23:42, 51). Strikingly, at the announcement of the birth of Jesus, the angel speaks of him as a great king: "He will be great, and will be called the Son of the Most High, and the Lord God will give to him the throne of his ancestor David. He will reign over the house of Jacob forever, and of his kingdom there will be no end" (1:32–34). That a literal kingdom was indeed expected by Jesus himself is clear from his words during the last supper: "I confer on you, just as my Father has conferred on me, a kingdom, so that you may eat and drink at my table in my kingdom, and you will sit on thrones judging the twelve tribes of Israel" (22:29–30). The embarrassment that the disciples were not sitting on thrones as judges over Israel further serves to confirm the literal expectation Jesus had concerning the coming of his kingdom. Thus, Jesus' message of good news to the poor consisted in announcing the coming kingdom of God, which differed starkly from the kingdoms of this world.

Significantly then, Jesus attitude toward the poor is centered on the Old Testament hope of the coming kingdom of God. In light of Luke's use of Isaiah, there are various other parallels that focus on God's attitude toward the poor. In Isaiah 3:14–15, God rises up in judgment against the powerful who crush the poor. Those who write laws meant to further oppress the poor he threatens with severe punishment (10:1–4). The poor and the meek are promised righteousness and equity, in apposition to the recompense of the wicked (11:4). As a more thorough study of the term πτωχός would reveal, it is used throughout the LXX in reference to the poor whom God favors. Significantly, some of these passages contain explicit directions in how the poor of the land are to be taken care of (e.g., Exod 23:6–11; Lev 23:22). Briefly put, the kingdom of God (which Jesus believed to be at hand) consisted in God's reign of righteousness. The oppression of the poor by the rich would come to an end. The poor would no longer be relegated to the outskirts of society. Conditions of slavery and indebtedness would end with the dawning of the new age. It is in the eschatological visions of the kingdom of God contained in the writings of Israel that Jesus' good news to the poor is properly understood.

Attempts to recast Jesus' message to the poor in metaphorical or spiritual terms would need to establish their case without ignoring the socio-economic and political context of first-century Palestine. This would bring the sharp contrast between rich and poor to the foreground of the Gospels. Lastly, by recovering Jesus' proclamation of the kingdom of God and comparing it to Second Temple literature, the good news to the poor offered in Jesus' message would surface with socio-economic implications, and not merely as the expectation of a future spiritual fulfillment. The kingdom that Jesus envisioned was one that would bring a radical transformation of the social, political, and economic conditions of his day: God would conduct a thorough reorganization of the world where his kingship would be established, a kingdom where justice would triumph over injustice, where poverty would be eliminated.

4

Divino Compañero

Toward a Hispanic Pentecostal Spirit-Christology

THE FIRST TWO CHAPTERS IN THIS WORK ARGUED THAT SPIRIT-Christology is a viable model for doing Christology in a distinctively Pentecostal way. The third chapter brought a necessary corrective—a Christology relevant to the specific community of Hispanic Pentecostals. Yet, though that chapter established the foundations for a contextual and liberative Christology, the move toward an actual Spirit-Christology that embodies these characteristics was not yet clearly articulated. In this chapter, I aim to weave together the different strands of christological reflection that I developed in the previous chapters with an understanding of Jesus developed from Hispanic Pentecostal spirituality.

Before embarking on this project, however, it is necessary to examine the context of Hispanic Pentecostals more closely. Yet, because there is much variation in the experience of Hispanic Pentecostals who reside in the U.S., this chapter focuses concretely on the Southwest Borderlands, where this author has lived for the past twenty-seven years, as a lens through which to understand the christological loci.

After the analysis of the context, I will turn to examining sources from which I will construct a Hispanic Pentecostal Christology, primarily the hymns and *coritos* that are sung in Pentecostal services. Though a clearer designation will be established later for the use of these songs, at this point all that needs to be said is that the reason for focusing on the songs is that they combine the testimonial aspect of the Hispanic Pentecostal experience as well as providing a canvas for interpretation. It is from these sources I propose to establish that Hispanic Pentecostals' experience of Jesus has always been understood as mediated by the Spirit, though it has never been theologically articulated. What becomes crucial toward this goal, however, is what parameters will be used to gauge authentically Pentecostal sources. Again, I will deal with this issue below.

The third section of this chapter will begin to construct a Spirit-Christology characterized by the spirituality of Hispanic Pentecostals' and their perception of Jesus as *El Divino Compañero* (the Divine Companion). I include in this christological reflection my own experience as an example and testimony of the reality of Hispanic Pentecostals, and the resulting view of Jesus. For the way Hispanic Pentecostals understand their experience of Jesus through the Spirit provides a pneumatic vision that reflects their particular contributions to Christology today.

The Hispanic Situation in the U.S.

In 1981, Isidro Lucas wrote a book entitled *The Browning of America*, which clearly traced the history, struggles, and aspirations of the Hispanics in the United States. According to the U.S. Census Bureau, the total Hispanic population in the U.S. had grown from 9 million in 1970 to 14.6 million in 1980, which accounted for 6.4 percent of the total U.S. population (226.5 million). Lucas argued that "the remarkable increase in the Hispanic population, coupled with their increasing awareness of their own characteristics, culture, and needs indicated that Hispanics could no longer be ignored, for they represent a new and vital force in the US and the church."[1] Today, according to the most recent statistics gathered by the U.S. Census Bureau in 2006, the Hispanic population was estimated at 44.3 million, which constituted about 14.8 percent of the total population of 299 million.[2] In addition, it must be pointed out that 60.1 percent of Hispanics residing in the U.S. are native born and of the other 39.1 percent who are foreign born at least half arrived here legally.[3] One other significant number to consider is that 11.5–12 million immigrants of Latin American descent (of which 78 percent come from Mexico) continue to live and work as illegal aliens.[4]

---

1. Lucas, *Browning of America*, 4.

2. U.S. Census Bureau, "Hispanic Population."

3. Much of the statistical data that follows is taken from a recent study of the Pew Hispanic Center, "Statistical Portrait of Hispanics."

4. Escobar, "Complex Tapestry of the Undocumented."

Although these statistics impressively show the rapid rate at which the Hispanic population is presently growing, the anticipated growth of the Hispanic population in the next 50 years as estimated by the U.S. Census Bureau is startling. Current projections estimate that by the year 2030 the Hispanic population will number 73 million, and 87.6 million by the year 2040. By the year 2050, Hispanics will become "the single largest minority group in the US, surpassing both the African-American and Asian-American populations."[5] Less than 5 decades from now, the Hispanic population is projected to grow to a staggering 102.6 million, which will consist of one-quarter of the predicted total U.S. population. Certainly, these figures pose a challenge to the church in the U.S. in general and Hispanic churches in particular because of the evangelistic challenge that Hispanics represent, but also for the theological academy.

Along with the significant rate of growth among Hispanics, it is also important to realize that close to 64 percent of the Hispanic population resides in only 4 states. California has the greatest number of Hispanics with 29.5 percent of the total U.S. Hispanic population, which accounts for a formidable 35.9 percent of the state's overall population. The state with the second largest Hispanic population is Texas, with 18.9 percent, which constitutes 35.6 percent of its population. The state of Florida follows with 8.2 percent, which is 20.1 percent of its population; and New York is the fourth, with 7.1 percent, which is 16.3 percent of its population.

Another factor with regard to the demographic aspects of the Hispanic population is urbanization. Approximately 87 percent of Hispanics living in the U.S. reside in major metropolitan areas. Of these an estimated 76.9 percent live in just 20 cities; 45.4 percent reside in Los Angeles (20.8 percent), New York (12 percent), Miami (4.7 percent), San Francisco/San Jose (4.1 percent), and Chicago (3.9 percent).

Moreover, Hispanics living in the U.S. represent 21 Latin American countries, which reveals a rich cultural and ethnic diversity among Hispanics. According to the U.S. Census the largest ethnic group among Hispanics is the Mexican population, which at an estimated 28.4 million represents 64.1 percent of the total Hispanic population. The second largest Hispanic group is Puerto Ricans, with almost 4 million, which

5. Mejido, "U.S. Hispanics/Latinos," 53–54.

makes up 9 percent of the Hispanic population. Hispanics of Cuban decent number 1.5 million, making them 3.4 percent of the Hispanic population.

The challenge that these demographics represent becomes even greater when one considers the social situation of the Hispanic population in the U.S. In this light, in the following paragraphs I survey the social conditions of the Hispanic community by briefly considering three factors: socioeconomic status, educational advancement, and political participation. These illuminate the social context in which Hispanics live and which Hispanic theology places its focus.

To understand the socioeconomic condition of the Hispanic population, we begin by looking at statistics regarding poverty and average personal/household income. An extraordinary 19.7 percent of Hispanic families live below the poverty line; an even more telling statistic is that 27.7 percent of Hispanic children live below the poverty line. With regard to average income, in 2006 the median annual personal earnings for Hispanics was $20,124, whereas for white Americans it was $30,186. The median household income figures also show a notable difference: $38,235 for Hispanic households and $51,920 for white households. What makes these statistics even more significant is the fact that Hispanic families are considerably larger in size, so family income has to be stretched much further than in most non-Hispanic households. What is more, these statistics do not account for those living in the U.S. illegally, who daily struggle to find work and food for their families.

Within this general demographic presentation of the Hispanic population of the U.S., Hispanic Pentecostals also have a particular ethos that is framed primarily by their experience as immigrants and the adverse economic situations that come from being unable to work legally at times, but also from having to work in low-paying jobs. It is not surprising to see that among the top occupations for Hispanics are the more menial and lowest paid, like in the hotel and restaurant industry, as well as cleaning and maintenance services. As one who has attended Hispanic Pentecostal church services in the U.S., I can vouch for the close relation there is between the social and economic ambivalence that the migratory status brings and how that in turn is reflected in the stories told as part of a testimony service, and the accompanying songs that many times were used to express those religious sentiments in light of the economic hardships incurred.

Hispanic Pentecostal's View of Jesus: Toward a Methodology

Within the matrix of existence presented above, Hispanic Pentecostals live and worship in close-knit communities that define their faith. Significantly, one has to consider how much the environment in which Hispanic Pentecostals live affects their religious understanding; for being Pentecostal provides an ethos of faith, but being Hispanic renders the context in which that faith is lived out.

Given the different experiences of the Spirit among Pentecostals, our theological understanding of the person of work of Jesus Christ, though distinctively pneumatologically oriented, may differ in emphasis from context to context. Early American Pentecostalism, for example, sought to overcome the challenge presented by the Oneness understanding of Jesus. Furthermore, their American context, specifically with regard to fundamentalism, informed their theological imagination. However, the questions brought to the Pentecostal systematician's table today are different due to our cultural locale and, hopefully, the resultant social concern for the community we live in. Thus, "thinking in the Spirit" about Jesus Christ is a major theme for Pentecostals. Yet, given the rich ethnic diversity due to our global presence, we need to approach Christology (as well as all other theological themes) conscious of the fact that our various contexts will undoubtedly enrich, sharpen, and probe our theological perspective.

Methodologically, I will focus primarily on how the Pentecostal experience informs our theological understanding. Since Pentecostalism from its origin has focused more on testimony, sermon, worship, and experience as sources for doing theology, it comes as no surprise that a Hispanic contribution might take the same contours. As Hispanic Pentecostals, the main resources that give shape to our theological imagination are testimony, sermon, and song. Yet all three of these necessarily pass through the filter of experience, and that experience is grounded in the struggle for life. As we listen to a sermon or song, our theological framework continues to be shaped. Our theology is not received simply through academic formation. Principally, as Kenneth Archer argues, the theological Pentecostal imagination is born out of the triadic engagement between Word, Spirit, and experience (both corporate and personal).[6]

6. Archer, *Pentecostal Hermeneutic*, ix.

In this respect, the considerations of non-Pentecostal Latina/o theologians are very much in line with our point of departure. Considering the critique and contribution that Latina/o theologians bring to the larger academy, Luis G. Pedraja incisively comments:

> Latina/o theologians are quite capable of engaging in critical and theoretical theological reflection à la Western European theoretical-rationalistic style that permeates current theological discussion. Most of us did it for our dissertations, and many of us still continue to make significant contributions in the field of systematic and philosophical theology. However, most of us recognize the need to go beyond Western European philosophical paradigms of theologizing and theorizing. Hence, Hispanic-Latina/o theology incorporates other aspects of theological reflection and other non-Western forms of rationality that are nevertheless essential components of theological reflections.[7]

The other aspects of theological reflection that he refers to here are: (1) "a noninnocent reading of Scriptures"; (2) critical assessment of the influence of power, politics, dominance, culture, and economic perspective on theological constructs; (3) to move beyond an abstract theology to one that values the lived experience of the community of faith and the culture one theologizes within; (4) for theology to become more than an exercise of thought and always move to action; (5) to voice the theology of the voiceless; and (6) for this to be a collaborative effort.

The way I perceive this Pentecostal imagination working is as follows. The Scriptures as interpreted in the Pentecostal community contain an experiential theology of the Spirit. Throughout the Old Testament and the New, the biblical authors reflect theologically on the experience of God in and through the Spirit, as encountered at Sinai or Pentecost, for example. In short, God manifests God's presence in history through a providential act on behalf of God's people or the world, and the biblical authors guided by the Spirit record primarily in narrative form the revelation of God given through that particular manifestation. In a sense, Pentecostals mirror that process as they think about what it means when God manifests his presence in a church service through a healing or a prophetic utterance in tongues. Their testimony about what God did makes a theological affirmation about who God is and what he is able to do through his Spirit today.

7. Pedraja, "Doing Theology in Spanish," 168.

What sort of Christology can we glean from the songs, testimonies, and sermons that are the main theological expressions of Hispanic Pentecostals? How does this understanding of Jesus Christ inform and expand the classic Pentecostal fivefold christological model (Savior, Sanctifier, Baptizer, Healer, and Soon-Coming King)? Briefly stated, Hispanic Pentecostals view Jesus as *El Divino Compañero*—their Divine Companion—the one who walks with them in midst of pain and struggle, and makes provision for their needs through his Spirit. I believe a pneumatologically oriented Christology is suitable for modeling an approach that stresses Jesus' divinity without jeopardizing his humanity. The Chalcedonian quest for understanding the essence and workings between the two natures of Christ was and is an important theological concern in Christology, especially among Hispanics. For example, Efrain Agosto comments,

> [T]he Chalcedonian definition of Jesus as fully human and fully divine makes sense to Latino theology because the humanity of Jesus ultimately identifies with our humanity, especially that of the poor and the oppressed. Moreover a fully human Jesus shows that God is God when God's full humanity is on display. If Jesus suffered and Jesus is fully God, then God suffers as we do.[8]

Yet, one has to recognize that although Agosto fleshes out this understanding from the ancient formula, historically, in its attempt to affirm categorically the divinity of Christ, Jesus' humanity and particularly his ministry and earthly works became almost insignificant when articulating the meaning of the person and nature of Jesus Christ.

In addition, Pentecostal theology with its pneumatological emphasis approaches the discussion inquiring about the activity of the Spirit in the life of Jesus—another aspect of Christology that the Chalcedonian formula is not interested in. For this reason, as has already been firmly established, Spirit-Christology is a better approach as it provides a more biblical and less philosophical framework for understanding Jesus as the Christ. Moreover, the work of Jesus Christ through the Spirit (yesterday and today) also becomes relevant. With this I simply contend that for a fuller christological treatment one has to ask about the ongoing and active ministry of Jesus Christ through his Spirit in the world and church

8. Agosto, "American (Hispanic) Christianity," 22–23.

today. Thus, from Jesus' birth to his resurrection, and through his continued work throughout church history, the relationship between Jesus and the Spirit is essential for understanding Jesus' nature and works.

The main contribution that Pentecostals bring to the Christological discussion is a pneumatological dimension that fuses together Christology and Pneumatology. Veli-Matti Kärkkäinen comments,

> Christology and Pneumatology are not only related but also interwoven in that, whatever Christ is, he is in the Spirit: Jesus Christ as the Savior, Healer, Sanctifier, Baptizer, and King. And conversely, whatever the Spirit effects in the believer's life, be it salvation, healing, sanctification baptism, or eschatological hope, it is the work of the Lord, Jesus Christ.[9]

From a Latina/o perspective, the anthropological aspect of Christology is stressed in order to highlight the fact that Jesus is the definition of what it means to be human. Samuel Solivan summarizes it like this: "Who Christ is in his humanity is fundamental for understanding who we are.... In the humanity of Jesus Christ, God has revealed what it is to be a true person. Hence, a Christian anthropology can be constructed only from a Christology."[10] God could have chosen His Son to be born in a palace with political power, thus placing him in a position to establish his kingdom.[11] Instead, he was born in a manger and lived his life as a poor Galilean prophet. Yet, he was not alone in this mission, for the Spirit accompanied him in his earthly mission from the incarnation to his resurrection. A Hispanic Pentecostal Christology, then, focuses on the liberating presence and praxis of Jesus' mission in the Spirit.

Significantly, though, if one were to go looking for Hispanic Pentecostal christological reflection in scholarly writings, such a search will inevitably yield few results, as I discovered when reviewing the theological works, periodical literature, and Sunday school material of the Hispanic ministry of the Church of God, Cleveland, Tennessee—La Iglesia de Dios. These sources tended to show a lack of original reflection from a Pentecostal perspective and typically merely restated a two-natures Chalcedonian Christology.

9. Kärkkäinen, "David's Sling," 152.

10. Solivan, *The Spirit, Pathos and Liberation*, 81.

11. Ibid., 83.

Yet there are two exceptions. The first is the widely read publication of Hiram Almirudis that serves as a study manual of the Church of God's Declaration of Faith within its Hispanic congregations.[12] In this study, the analysis of Jesus' divinity and humanity simply affirms evangelical doctrines of the incarnation, the kenosis, and the atonement theories. The second is a book published by the Church of God's Hispanic publishing house, Editorial Evangélica. This book was conceived as a manual for biblical doctrine and practical Christian living. Yet, once again the analysis of the person and work of Jesus departs from an evangelically oriented theology, as can be recognized by following the bibliographic trail of its sources.[13] My analysis of the periodicals *El Evangelio* and *La Senda Iluminada*,[14] as wells as the Sunday School lesson guide *El Maestro Pentecostés* yielded similar results.[15]

In light of this lack of academic resources on Christology, a better approach would be to analyze Hispanic Pentecostals' popular theology, particularly that found in their testimonies and songs. For in order to understand their distinctive christological contributions, as Eldin Villafañe states, "it would be much more fruitful and in a real sense closer to its indigenous nature to look at the *implicit theology* manifested, above all, in the 'culto.'"[16] By "culto" Villafañe refers to the Hispanic Pentecostal service in general and specifically to the activities within the service that serve to express the implicit theological discourse; for

12. Almirudis, *Comentario Sobre la Declaración*. I had the privilege of working with this author in my days at the Hispanic Institute of Ministry. Moreover, I read and typeset the original manuscripts at the author's request before it went on to publication. This book is a condensed version of Hiram Almirudis doctoral thesis, entitled "A Commentary on the Church of God Declaration of Faith for Latin American Churches."

13. Calderón, ed. *Doctrina Bíblica*.

14. The following articles are representative of the christological reflection in these periodicals: Betancourt, "La Primera Navidad"; Camacho, "Jesus … ¡Hijo del Altisimo!"; Santos, "La Verdad de la Navidad"; and Ramos, "La Sencillez de la Encarnación." Interestingly, and appropriately, these articles were all written during the Christmas season.

15. The following lesson plans also reveal the typical lack of Pentecostal distinctives: Calderón, "La Divinidad de Jesucristo" and "La humanidad de Jesucristo"; Calderón, "Cristo, el Hijo de Dios"; Rivera, ed., "El Dios Encarnado"; and Miranda, ed., "Jesús, el Verbo Hecho Carne."

16. Villafañe, *Liberating Spirit*, 123.

example, sermons, testimonies, songs, and any other activity practiced by the "community of the Spirit" in or outside the church walls.[17]

Yet because of the extemporaneous nature of Pentecostal worship, it is very difficult to gather and document the resources needed for such a theological investigation. For example, there is no hymnal that consists of only songs composed by Hispanic Pentecostals. And then there is the question of how to determine whether a particular source can be considered to be Pentecostal. The difficulty of this process can be seen when one considers that many hymns (and *coritos*) were adopted either verbatim or at times with an added Pentecostal slant, and that they were not necessarily written by Pentecostals, but were adopted because they in some way express the Pentecostal experience. In fact a large percentage of hymns sung in Hispanic Pentecostal churches were translated from their Anglo counterparts or borrowed from Hispanic Apostolic hymnals. [18]

The justification for using the hymns and *coritos* that follow therefore stems from two realizations. On the one hand, it is very common in the traditional Hispanic Pentecostal service for a brother or sister to take the pulpit and offer a testimony, which is then followed by a hymn that goes with what was just said. A personal example of this is from my recollection of my parents'—Quirino and Alicia Alfaro—testimony. One of the two would go to the pulpit and testify and then ask the other to join them with a special song for the Lord. Likewise, as part of my research, I came into the possession of Abundio Saldivar's (my father-in-law) rustic notebook/hymnbook. As typical of many Pentecostal psalmists who sing to the Lord, he carried that hymnbook with him and wrote down in it the songs he heard that had a special significance and meaning for his experience of walking with the Lord.

It was in his hymnbook that I found evidence for the sort of borrowing mentioned above. Some songs are translations of a classic Pentecostal or evangelical hymn. Others are taken from the repertoire of Hispanic composers. Yet, the most dear to his heart—the ones that were sung the most—and the ones which more characteristically evoke some Hispanic Pentecostal sentiment were those that, unbeknownst to my father-in-law, where penned by one of many Mexican Oneness

17. Ibid., 121.

18. For a statistical study of Latino hymnody with a special focus on Pentecostal hymnody, see Ramirez, "Alabaré a mi Señor."

Pentecostals. This suggests that authorship is less significant than content; what is important to the singer is the song's resonance with his or her experience and its ability to transport the singer to a plane where her or his experience is interconnected with the words of the song.

In the pages that follow I will trace the main contours of the christological reflection contained in the songs, but because of the simplicity of the hymns' language I will not provide extended "exegetical" analyses of the hymns or *coritos*; it is simply not necessary or particularly illuminating. What follows then is more of a descriptive outline that seeks to substantiate a christological foundation that flows out from the wells of Hispanic Pentecostal spirituality.

The Jesus of Hispanic Pentecostal Spirituality

First of all, the miracle-working Jesus is a dominant part of the Hispanic Pentecostal christological imagination. In light of the economic hardships, it is not surprising that Hispanic Pentecostals turn to Jesus as the doctor *par excellence*. Take for instance this very popular *corito*:

This Is the Christ[19]

This is the Christ, that I preach
and I don't get tired of preaching
He heals the sick,
Rebukes the demons,
And calms the storm.

In the same vein, but more telling of the relation between Jesus and the Spirit is the following:

Pass through Here Lord

Pass through here Lord,
pass through here
Oh, Oh Lord, pass through here
Holy Spirit, fill me with you
Oh, oh Lord, fill me with you

---

19. In order to provide documentary evidence for Hispanic Pentecostal's understanding of Jesus, I have taken the liberty of translating various popular *coritos* and hymns from Spanish into English. To my knowledge, none of these songs have been previously translated in print, therefore, I take full responsibility, and apologize, for the rustic non-lyrical style, employed for the sole purpose of conveying meaning.

In this sense, Hispanic Pentecostals juxtapose the presence of Jesus and the Spirit, indicating that manner in which Jesus' presence is manifested through the Spirit. Three other *coritos* express a very similar connection between Jesus' presence in the church through the Spirit.

We Are One in the Spirit

We are one in the Spirit
we are one in the Lord
and they will know we are one
by his love, by his love
and they will know we are one
by his love

The Song of the Spirit

Oh, let the Lord
in his Spirit of love,
satisfy today your heart and soul
surrender what he requests
and his Spirit will come
Over you, giving you new life.

Christ Is in This Meeting

Christ is in this meeting
he has promised to be here
where two or three
in my name are gathered
there I will be, there I will be
there I will be

I feel him in me
his Spirit makes me talk
I feel him in me
his Spirit makes me sing
And I will praise him
with all my heart
and I will preach
saying glory to God

All three of these *coritos* suggest the work of Jesus as being in and through the Spirit. Thus, every Pentecostal/Charismatic manifestation that one may experience is ultimately understood as being closely connected to Jesus and the Spirit.

Another facet of the sort of christological reflection that can be gleaned from Hispanic Pentecostal's hymn preferences is the absolute humanity of Jesus. The portrait of Jesus that the following hymns present is of a bloody and mutilated Jesus on the cross, dying; but they depict him not as mere man but as God. From reading the following two hymns one gets a sense of the deep understanding of Jesus' suffering to the point where one cannot sing these melodies without shedding a tear.

DIVINE FACE

Divine face, bloodied up
Body mutilated for our good;
Benign calm, just anger,
The eyes that see you like this cry.

Precious hands, so hurt,
Nailed to a cross for my sake;
In this valley be my guide,
And my happiness, my northstar and light.
Beautiful side, in which wound,
Humanity finds life;
Loving fountain, of a clement God
Eloquent voice of charity

Your wounded feet, patient Christ
Indifferently I hammered them;
And repentant today I worship you
I implore your grace; Lord, I sinned.

Crucified, on a wooden beam,
Meek Lamb, you die for me;
That is why the saddened soul
Anxiously longs, Lord, for you.

HE SUFFERED AGONY

The Lord of the universe suffered agony
When the traitor betrayed him with a kiss
Being whipped by those men
While beaten he asked for their forgiveness.

Chorus
In my dream I saw that they whipped you
I ran Lord to defend you
But the man who I thought was another
Upon seeing his face, Lord, I saw mine.

In the heavens lives the One we worship
There is the work of man and his hands
They're wounds of the spear and the nails
The wounds he suffered to save us.

The thorns sunk in his forehead
and his face all disfigured
and suffering to the point of death
He took upon himself the burden of sin.

This last song underscores the typical Pentecostal experience of being inspired by a dream. Moreover it also hints at the kenotic understanding of Jesus' pre-existence and his giving up of that state to become one with humanity; he was the Lord of the universe and despite that he suffered great agony, all for our sake. Two more songs serve to highlight the emphasis on the kenosis:

Thank You God

Thank you God, thank you God
for your love and your goodness
thank you God, thank you God
for the gift of preaching salvation
Being God he did not care
he gave himself for you and me
Emptying himself he became humble

Lamb

Lamb who descended from heaven
to die on the cross,
to give me light
And also salvation

You shed your immaculate blood,
With which my wickedness,
By dying on the cross
Jesus, You forgave

Today I worship You
With all of my heart
Because you are my God
and my good Savior
who died for me
who died for me

Another important characteristic of Hispanic Pentecostal Christology as understood from this particular social context is the idea that Jesus is the answer for all that troubles humanity. Not just sin, but even the social problems of the world find their remedy in Jesus.

CHRIST IS THE ANSWER

Christ is the answer
for the world today
like him there is no one else
Christ is the Lord

If you have problems
in the depth of your soul
if you have a thousand questions
which you can't answer
accept Jesus Christ
he will help you
and then to your questions
he will respond

Significantly, this next song places the evils of the world in a personal perspective (addictions one is hard pressed to overcome), but also demonstrates a more systemic understanding of evil as the cause of injustice and prejudice. To both these ills the remedy that God has given is Jesus Christ.

THE REMEDY OF GOD

When you can see in all the world
the effects of evil everywhere
when you can see that the carnal man
cannot leave his vices behind

Chorus
The remedy of God
is Christ Jesus
it's Jesus Christ the Lord

When you can see social injustice
is the cause of so much suffering
when racial prejudices flourish
it's the infernal flower of error

The following hymn not only brings together the personal experience of Jesus through the Spirit in a way that incorporates the themes elaborated above, but also hints at the social ramifications of a Christ who descends from his throne to be part of a poor family, and in that humility brings the world liberty and salvation.

A PLACE FOR CHRIST

You left your throne and crown for me
By coming to Bethlehem to be born;
But you were not given entrance to the inn
And you were made to be born in a stable.

Chorus
Come to my heart, oh Christ!
For there is a place for you;
Come to my heart, oh Christ!, come,
For there is a place for you.

Heavenly praises the angels given
Offering praise to the Word
But you humbly came to earth, Lord,
To give life to the worst of sinners.

The foxes can have their caves,
and the birds their nests;
But the Son of man did not have a place
Upon which to rest his head.

You came, Lord, with your great blessing
To give liberty and salvation;
But with hatred and scorn they killed you,
Although they saw your love and virtue.

Divino Compañero: A Pentecostal Contribution to Hispanic Christology

The above analysis leaned heavily on the content of the songs presented to illustrate the christological imagination that inspires Hispanic Pentecostals. Building on this, I now turn to an exploration of some personal sources for a Hispanic Pentecostal Christology from my own experience as an immigrant to the U.S. Let me begin by retelling some stories that serve as foundational to my christological reflection, for I believe that Hispanic Pentecostal theology is best expressed in a medium that is similar to its nature: narrative. There are three short anecdotes that serve to frame what I believe forms part of the Hispanic Pentecostal christological imagination.

The first comes from my childhood in Mexico. One of the earliest church-related memories that I have is that of sitting with other children in the midst of a circle of adults who were playing guitars and singing praises to the Lord. A song that stands out from those impromptu worship sessions at someone's house is "*Divino Compañero*." The reason it has been engraved in my memory is because the song expresses the immanent presence of Jesus in the Christian's pilgrimage while on this earth. The song's chorus makes a clear allusion to the biblical passage where Jesus catches up to some of his disciples on the way to Emmaus (Luke 24:13–32); there is a melancholy plea for the Lord to stay with them and to make their hearts his permanent residence.[20]

DIVINE COMPANION OF THE WAY

Divine companion of the way
your presence I feel as I walk
Christ has dissipated all shadow
I now have light, the divine light of his love

Chorus
Stay, Lord, it's getting late
I offer you my heart to inhabit
make it you permanent dwelling place
accept it, accept it, my Savior

The shadow of the night is nearing
and in it the tempter looms
don't leave me alone on the path
help me, help me until I arrive

After living in Toluca, Mexico, for three years, we immigrated to the U.S., and in one of our last gatherings with the brothers and sisters from church this song was sung. With tears in theirs eyes the adults played this song as if not wanting it to end because our journey would soon begin. Later, when we got situated in Phoenix and began to attend a Pentecostal church, my parents would regularly sing this song during the testimony service. As a theologian, I now reflect on the meaning the song had for them; indeed, "*El Divino Compañero*" had been with them on their northward journey. I believe that one could very well document

---

20. I have been unable to document this, but Daniel Ramirez let me know that this song was composed by a Mexican Apostolic (Pentecostal) man who had been deported from the U.S.

very similar experiences of the accompanying presence of Jesus when sharing stories of our migratory pilgrimage. Throughout our journey, and even now, Jesus has been our constant friend and companion who has never let us down.

A second anecdote comes from a rather recent realization I came to while having a conversation with an aunt (my father's sister). She informed me that while living in the border town of San Luis, Sonora, my grandfather entered the *Bracero* program[21] and it was during that time that he converted to Pentecostalism. When I remember my "Tata" (as we affectionately called him) today I form an image in my mind of a rugged man whose skin had become darker and more wrinkled from working long hours in the hot sun. Yet, I also imagine him going about his work days in the Arizona and California deserts joyfully because of the Pentecostal praises in his heart and on his lips.

Another quick flashback that serves to frame the Hispanic Pentecostal christological imagination is an incident that took place in the early eighties. One hot summer day a man knocked at our door. My mom spoke to him and he turned out to be a Salvadoran refugee who had come to the end of his resources. He was pleading for food and a place to stay; my parents gave him both and helped him find a job.

In many ways these three anecdotes comprise one of the main facets of the Hispanic religious experience. Speaking from a Southwest borderlands immigrant perspective, we were formed, and continue to be formed, by the struggles of the immigrant journey. While living here in a state of ambivalence, of being *ni de aquí ni de allá* ("neither from here nor from there") and struggling to adapt to American culture, the experience of Hispanics in general, and those living in the Southwest borderlands in particular, can best be described as "unempowered."[22] From this "underempowered" position, various religious strategies have been put in place implicitly or explicitly in order to ameliorate the living conditions of our "alien" status. For Hispanic Pentecostals, this strategy includes walking in the presence of their Lord and Savior through the Spirit.

---

21. An immigrant worker program that allowed up to 250,000 Mexican laborers to work in the U.S. between 1942 and 1964.

22. Avalos, *Introduction to the U.S. Latina and Latino Religious Experience*, 300–301.

In the immigrant Hispanic Pentecostal experience, there is an image that may serve to capture their religious experience of Jesus: *El Coyote Místico* (The Mystic Coyote)—for ultimately he guided their journey.[23] As Pentecostal immigrants who have come to the U.S. can testify, Jesus accompanied them on their pilgrimage. On the nights when darkness and solitude tempted them to go back, he was their light and encouragement. On the days when the scorching sun threatened their lives and impeded their progress, he was their shelter and refreshment. Facing the danger of death in the hands of the evil *coyotes*, *El Coyote Místico* protected them when they had no one else to turn to or trust. He fed them and gave them water to drink, and above all, he gave to them the living water of faith to sustain them and help them finish their journey. Daniel Ramirez documents one such testimony of the activity of Christ the Mystic Coyote.

> [O]n the drive up Interstate Highway 5 from San Diego under overcast skies, a *coyote* noticed that his two middle-aged matronly *pollitas* had that unmistakable look of *aleluyas* (Holy Rollers). Their conservative attire; make-up-free faces, and tied-back and uncut hair betrayed their identity.
>
> "Looks like you're Christians, right?" "Yes, Sir," came the nervous reply.
>
> "Well, start praying for rain. When there's rain, the agents at the San Onofre station go indoors and stop checking the cars."
>
> Drawing from deep reservoirs, Hermana Godínez and her companion clasped hands and prayed in the words of the old *corito*: "Manda la lluvia, Señor!" (Send down the rain, Lord!). As they sped past San Onofre and toward Los Angeles and church and kin, the only *mojados* (wetbacks) were the Border Patrol agents seeking refuge from the downpour.[24]

Testimonies like these abound in both Pentecostal and non-Pentecostal Hispanic congregations. As in the stories of the Bible that reveal the providential care of God, the immigrants who come to the U.S. are not alone in their journeys. Christ is the Guide and Shepherd of those who

---

23. *El Coyote* is someone who gets paid to guide immigrants across the border. I first heard of the concept with reference to Christ from Daniel Ramírez, who spoke at the West Regional Conference of the Hispanic Theological Initiative on February 28, 2004.

24. Ramirez, "Public Lives in American Hispanic Churches," 186.

make the dangerous journey to come to the U.S.; he is their Divine Companion.

Toward a Hispanic Pentecostal Spirit-Christology

But what are the implications of this experiential approach to Christology when approached from the model of Spirit-Christology? What insight does the experience of Jesus through the Spirit in the midst of an adverse economic situation or in light of unjust migratory policies yield? On the one hand it speaks of Jesus' identification with the sufferer, and on the other hand it empowers them for seeking avenues of social change.

Though traditionally it has been thought that Pentecostalism opts for a pie-in-the-sky theology that ignores social context, this Spirit-Christology seeks to address the issue from the perspective of Jesus the Spirit-anointed social prophet. Having drunk too long from other wells, primarily from the fundamentalist and more recently from the evangelical, it is time for Hispanic Pentecostals to draw inspiration from their own sources, which will provide a much needed *pneumatic* contribution to the U.S. Latina/o understanding of Jesus presented in the previous chapter.

As we venture forward toward the construction of a Pentecostal Christology, our point of departure should be the active presence of Jesus in his church through the Spirit. If ultimately Jesus' life defines what it means to be human and his presence today is mediated through the Spirit, is not our christological model of Savior, Sanctifier, Healer, Baptizer, and Coming King limited? Do we not need to expand this foundational model to include others that rightly highlight the social dimensions of the gospel? Should we not aim to have a "fuller" gospel, a gospel that has a more holistic view of Jesus' life and mission?

Given the social context of Hispanic Pentecostal churches, we cannot afford to ignore the economic and marginalized condition of our communities. Ours is not a question of opting for the poor, as if they were alien to our community. The physical location of our churches, their strategic position within the *barrios* (or ghettos) of the U.S., and the social status of our congregants demand a Pentecostal theology that is committed to a holistic view of salvation that includes righteousness and justice, redemption from sin as well as sinful social structures, physical and emotional health, and also social and economic well-being.

In part the road toward a holistic Pentecostal theology has already been paved, but we need to expand it. By this, I mean that we need to reinterpret our christocentric fivefold gospel from a corporate and not merely an individualistic understanding. For Jesus is not just our personal Savior; he is the Redeemer of the world. Jesus is not just our personal Sanctifier; he yearns to bring corporate sanctification to the church and society. He is not just our personal Healer, but also the One who can deliver all people from every social evil. He does not baptize us with his Spirit for our own personal enjoyment; he does so to send us out on a Spirit-led mission to the poor and the oppressed. Lastly, Christ is not just our Coming King; but the Proclaimer of God's reign among us—a reign that does not operate only in the spiritual dimension, but that denounces injustice and demands a praxis of love and justice. I believe that such a vision can be undertaken and put to practice as we wrestle with the meaning of the life and mission of Jesus in the power of the Spirit.

Conclusion

Over the years that I have been working on this project, I have spoken to church leaders, pastors, and fellow Pentecostal believers about the ins and outs of my book. After explaining the theoretical intricacies that my argument entails, I have regularly been confronted with the comment, "Yeah, but does it preach." Fleshing out what this means, the following question surges: What use is a model for Spirit-Christology if it has no practical application for the Pentecostal church and the believer? Seeking to respond to this "so what" attitude, I conclude that Spirit-Christology provides a christological model that is not only useful for understanding the person and work of Jesus, but is also a tool for tempering some of the excesses that have resulted within Pentecostal and Charismatic Christianity when an emphasis on the Spirit is stressed over against christological themes.

In light of the unprecedented growth of the prosperity gospel and its appeal to Hispanic Pentecostals, it is vital that some words of caution might be offered from a christological perspective as developed in this study. The seriousness of the issue could perhaps be underestimated from an outsider's point of view, but anyone who is actively engaged in church ministry in a Hispanic Pentecostal congregation can affirm the grave dangers this movement impinges upon them in light of their socio-economic situation.

The prosperity movement has subtly advanced the idea that Jesus was a rich man; that he lived and died surrounded by riches and for that reason we too can live a life of luxury and abundance. The sad part of this affirmation is that many Hispanic Pentecostals who are experiencing economic crisis have bought into it. After hearing a message from an "anointed prophet," they not only believe this false representation of Jesus, but also send their sacrificial offerings with the hope that by sowing a faith seed their finances will improve. Thousands and thouands of sincere Charismatic and Pentecostal believers in the U.S. and worldwide continue to send their offerings faithfully thinking that their contributions will reap an abundant blessing with which they will pay of their debts and turn their financial crisis around. Sadly they are victims of a theological fraud that has only made the teachers of this "gospel" rich.

Let me offer then some corrective comments that flow from the gist of my argument and serve to highlight the main conclusions of this proposal. First of all, because Pentecostal have always had a paradigmatic concern for looking back to Jesus, it is imperative to have a careful understanding of who Jesus was in his historical manifestation before applying his Spirit-led mission to our lives. In many ways, a paradigmatic understanding of Jesus that is focused only on the power and not also the presence of the Holy Spirit in the life of Jesus may lead to a Christian life that is incoherent. To live in the power of the Spirit today is also to live in the presence of the sanctifying Spirit that guided Jesus' life and work.

Second, if Jesus is our model *par excellence* for living in the Spirit, he is also our example of ministry in the Spirit. As such, our focus should be to try to imitate Jesus and his Pentecostal mission, with an integral view of salvation that includes all the spheres of life that need to be transformed. On the one hand, this means to envision a charismatic ministry that offers healing—spiritual as well as physical and emotional. On the other hand, it means to bring the prophetic role of ministry to encompass not just the realm of the spoken word (preaching, prophesying, speaking in tongues) but also the social dimension of seeking the justice of God's kingdom.

Lastly, for Hispanic Pentecostals, Spirit-Christology provides a balanced interpretative model that bridges our heritage with new visions for Pentecostal understanding. There is no need to throw out the classical beliefs of our tradition or simply attach them as appendices to our evangelical doctrinal views. There is a sense in which we can rethink our tradition in light of the Spirit in a way that is even more Pentecostal than at the beginning of the Pentecostal movement. This may in turn provide the theological method and framework that is missing in Pentecostal theology, and that is so very needed in our churches to guard against doctrinal error as we seek to understand the Bible from a distinctly pneumatological perspective.

Bibliography

Agosto, Efrain. "American (Hispanic) Christianity." In *Jesus in History, Thought, and Culture: An Encyclopedia*, edited by Leslie Houlden, 1:20–25. Santa Barbara: ABC Clio, 2003.

Aiken, W.T. "The Bride and the Bridegroom." *CGE* 12:12 (1921) 3.

Alexander, Kimberly Ervin. *Pentecostal Healing: Models in Theology and Practice.* JPTSup 29. Blandford Forum, UK: Deo, 2006.

Allen, David. "Regent Square Revisited: Edward Irving—Precursor of the Pentecostal Movement." *Journal of the European Pentecostal Theological Association* 17 (1997) 49–58.

Almirudis, Hiram. "A Commentary on the Church of God Declaration of Faith for Latin American Churches." DMin thesis, San Francisco Theological Seminary, 1981.

———. *Comentario Sobre la Declaración de Fe de la Iglesia de Dios.* San Antonio: H. Almirudis, 1997.

Althouse, Peter. "Toward a Theological Understanding of the Pentecostal Appeal to Experience." *Journal of Ecumenical Studies* 38 (2001) 399–411.

Alvarez, Carmelo. "Hispanic Pentecostals: Azusa Street and Beyond." *Cyberjournal for Pentecostal-Charismatic Research* 5 (February 1999). Online: http://www.pctii .org/cyberj/cyberj5/alvarez.html.

———. "Latin American Pentecostals: Ecumenical and Evangelical." *Pneuma* 9 (Spring 1987) 91–95.

———, editor. *Pentecostalismo y Liberación: Una Experiencia Latinoamericana.* Colección Tradición Protestante. San José: Editorial Departamento de Investigaciones, 1992.

Anderson, Allan. *An Introduction to Pentecostalism: Global Charismatic Christianity.* Cambridge: Cambridge University Press, 2004.

Anderson, Allan, and Edmond Tang, editors. *Asian and Pentecostal: The Charismatic Face of Christianity in Asia.* Baguio City, Philippines: APTS, 2005.

Aquino, Jorge A. "The Prophetic Horizon of Latino Theology." In *Rethinking Latino(a) Religion and Identity*, edited by Miguel A. De La Torre and Gastón Espinosa, 101–28. Cleveland: Pilgrim, 2006.

Archer, Kenneth J. *A Pentecostal Hermeneutic for the Twenty-First Century: Spirit, Scripture and Community.* JPTSup 28. London: T. & T. Clark, 2004.

———. "Pentecostal Story: The Hermeneutical Filter for the Making of Meaning." *Pneuma* 26 (Spring 2004) 36–59.

Arrington, French L. *Christian Doctrine: A Pentecostal Perspective.* 3 vols. Cleveland, TN: Pathway, 1992–94.

———. "The Use of the Bible by Pentecostals." *Pneuma* 16 (Spring 1994) 101–8.

Assmann, Hugo. "The Power of Christ in History: Conflicting Christologies and Discernment." In *Frontiers of Theology in Latin America*, edited by Rosino Gibellini, translated by John Drury, 134–45. Maryknoll, NY: Orbis, 1975.

———. *Teología Desde la Praxis de la Liberación: Ensayo Teológico Desde la América Dependiente* . Salamanca: Sígueme, 1971.

Avalos, Hector, editor. *Introduction to the U.S. Latina and Latino Religious Experience*. Religion in the Americas 2. Boston: Brill Academic, 2004.

Baker, E.V. "The Bride of Christ." *BM* 61 (May 1, 1910) 1, 4.

Barney, Jesse A. "Statement of Doctrine." *BM* 229 (April 1921) 4.

Barrett, D. B., and T. M. Johnson. "Global Statistics," In *NIDPCM*, 284–302.

Barth, Hattie M. "Healing in the Atonement." *BM* 275 (January–March 1930) 1–2.

Barth, Karl. "Evangelical Theology in the 19th Century." In *The Humanity of God*. Richmond: John Knox, 1972.

Bayerhaus, E. "The Birth of Christ and Its Message to Us." *PE* 577 (December 20, 1924) 4.

Beall, R.B. "The Holy Spirit as a Person." *Pentecostal Holiness Advocate* 1:3 (1917) 2–3.

Bell, E. N. "Who Is Jesus Christ?" *PE* 103 (August 14, 1915) 1.

Bernard, K. David. *The Oneness of God*. Series in Pentecostal Theology 1. Hazelwood, MO: Word Aflame, 2000.

———. *The Oneness View of Jesus Christ*. Hazelwood, MO: Word Aflame, 1994.

Betancourt, Esdras. "La Primera Navidad." *El Evangelio* 36:12 (December 1981) 4–5.

Bevans, Stephen B. *Models of Contextual Theology*. Faith and Cultures. Maryknoll, NY: Orbis, 1992.

Bevins, Winfield H. *Rediscovering John Wesley*. Cleveland: Pathway, 2004.

Boddy, A. A. "The Holy Ghost for Us." *PE* 205 (September 1, 1917) 1.

Boff, Leonardo. *Jesus Christ Liberator: A Critical Christology for Our Time*. Translated by Patrick Hughes. Maryknoll, NY: Orbis, 1978.

Bonino, José Míguez, editor. *Faces of Jesus: Latin American Christologies*. Translated by Robert R. Barr. Maryknoll, NY: Orbis, 1984.

Bosworth, F. F. *Christ the Healer*. Grand Rapids: Revell, 1973 [1924].

Boudewijnse, Barbara, André Droogers, and Frans Kamsteeg, editors. *Algo Más que Opio: Una Lectura Antropológica del Pentacostalismo Latinoamericano y Caribeño*. Colección Sociología de la Religión. San Jose: Departamento Ecuménico de Investigaciones, 1991.

Boyd, Gregory A. *Oneness Pentecostals and the Trinity*. Grand Rapids: Baker, 1992.

Brewster, P. S., editor. *Pentecostal Doctrine*. Cheltenham, UK: Grenehurst, 1976.

Bridges, Laura. "Jesus Is Her Healer." *CGE* 12:42 (1921) 3.

Brown, Colin. *Miracles and the Critical Mind*. Grand Rapids: Eerdmans, 1984.

———. "The Role of the Spirit in the Conception of Jesus." Unpublished paper, 2003.

Bueno, Daniel Ruiz. *Padres Apostólicos*. Madrid: Biblioteca de Autores Cristianos, 1993.

Bundy, David. "Boddy, Alexander Alfred." In *NIDPCM*, 436–37.

———. "Irving, Edward." In *NIDPCM*, 803–4.

Burgess, Stanley M., editor. *Encyclopedia of Pentecostal and Charismatic Christianity*. New York: Routledge, 2006.

Bussmann, Claus. *Who Do You Say? Jesus Christ in Latin American Theology.* Translated by Robert R. Barr. Maryknoll, NY: Orbis, 1985.

Butler, Daniel L. *Oneness Pentecostalism: A History of the Jesus Name Movement.* Bellflower, CA: International Pentecostal Church, 2004.

Calderón, Wilfredo. "Cristo, el Hijo de Dios." *El Maestro Pentecostés* 40:7 (1990–1991) 5–11.

———. "La Divinidad de Jesucristo." *El Maestro Pentecostés* 48:14 (1994) 5–11.

———, editor. *Doctrina Bíblica y Vida Cristiana.* Cleveland, TN: Editorial Evangélica, 1994.

———. "La Humanidad de Jesucristo." *El Maestro Pentecostés* 48:14 (1994) 12–18.

Camacho, Héctor. "Jesus . . . ¡Hijo del Altisimo!" *El Evangelio* 19:12 (1984) 3–5.

Campos, Bernardo. "El Pentecostalismo en la Fuerza del Espíritu." *Cyberjournal for Pentecostal-Charismatic Research* 9 (February 2001). Online: http://www.pctii .org/cyberj/cyberj9/campos.html

Cartledge, Mark J. *Practical Theology: Charismatic and Empirical Perspectives.* Carlisle, UK: Paternoster, 2003.

Cashwell, Gaston B. "Our Lord's Finished Work." *BM* 104 (February 15, 1912) 1.

Castelo, Daniel. "Tarrying on the Lord: Affections, Virtues and Theological Ethics in Pentecostal Perspective." *JPT* 13:1 (2004) 31–56.

Chan, Simon. *Pentecostal Theology and the Christian Spiritual Tradition.* JPTSup 21. Sheffield: Sheffield Academic, 2000.

Charette, Blaine. *Restoring Presence: The Spirit in Matthew's Gospel.* JPTSup 18. Sheffield: Sheffield Academic, 2000.

Childers, J. C. "Jesus the Only Healer." *CGE* 13:39 (1922) 3.

Chiquete, Daniel, and Luis Orellana, editors. *Voces del Pentecostalismo Latinoamericano: Identidad, Teología e Historia.* Concepción: RELEP, 2003.

Christenson, Larry. "Pentecostalism's Forgotten Forerunner." In *Aspects of Pentecostal-Charismatic Origins,* edited by Vinson Synan, 17–37. Plainfield: Logos, 1975.

Cleary, Edward L., and Hannah W. Stewart-Gambino, editors. *Power, Politics, and Pentecostals in Latin America.* Boulder, CO: Westview, 1997.

Coleman, Simon. *The Globalization of Charismatic Christianity: Spreading the Gospel of Prosperity.* Cambridge Studies in Ideology and Religion 12. Cambridge: Cambridge University Press, 2000.

"Combined Minutes of the General Council of the Assemblies of God." 8th ed. Springfield, MO, September 21–27, 1920.

Cook, Michael L. "Jesus from the Other Side of History: Christology in Latin America." *Theological Studies* 44:2 (1983) 258–87.

Copley, A. S. *Liberty of the Sons of God: Lessons on Galatians.* Kansas City: Grace and Glory, 1914.

———. "Pentecost in Type." *The Pentecost* 1:8 (1908) 7–8.

———. "Power from On High, I." *BM* 2:26 (1908) 2.

———. "Power from On High, II." *BM* 2:27 (1908) 4.

———. "The Prayer of the Just." *BM* 35 (1909) 2.

———. "Why We Need the Baptism." *BM* 2:31 (1909) 2.

Corten, André, and Ruth Marshall-Fratani, editors. *Between Babel and Pentecost: Transnational Pentecostalism in Africa and Latin America.* Bloomington: Indiana University Press, 2000.

Costas, Orlando E. *Christ outside the Gate: Mission beyond Christendom*. Maryknoll, NY: Orbis, 1982.

Cotnam, R. L. "Sanctification, or the Blood Applied." *CGE* 9:49 (1918) 2.

Cotton, Lorena. "The Bride of Christ." *CGE* 18:29 (1927) 2.

———. "The Holy Spirit and His Work." *CGE* 14:39 (1923) 4.

Cox, Harvey G. *Fire from Heaven: The Rise of Pentecostal Spirituality and the Reshaping of Religion in the Twenty-First Century*. Reading, MA: Addison-Wesley, 1995.

Cross, Terry L. "A Review of Ben Witherington, *The Problem with Evangelical Theology: Testing the Exegetical Foundations of Calvinism, Dispensationalism and Wesleyanism*." Paper presented at the 36th annual meeting of the Society of Pentecostal Studies. Cleveland, TN, March 9, 2007.

Dabney, D. Lyle. "Saul's Armor: The Problem and the Promise of Pentecostal Theology Today." *Pneuma* 23 (Spring 2001) 115–46.

———. "Why Should the Last Be First?: The Priority of Pneumatology in Recent Theological Discussion." In *Advents of the Spirit: An Introduction to the Current Study of Pneumatology*, edited by Bradford E. Hinze and D. Lyle Dabney, 238–59. Marquette Studies in Theology 30. Milwaukee: Marquette University Press, 2001.

Dallimore, Arnold. *The Life of Edward Irving: Forerunner of the Charismatic Movement*. Chicago: Moody, 1983.

Daniels, David D. "Dialogue between Black and Hispanic Pentecostal Scholars: A Report and Some Personal Observations." *Pneuma* 17 (Fall 1995) 219–28.

Davids, P. H. "Rich and Poor." In *Dictionary of Jesus and the Gospels*, edited by Joel B. Green and Scot McKnight, 701–10. Downers Grove, IL: InterVarsity, 1992.

Dayton, Donald W. *Theological Roots of Pentecostalism*. Studies in Evangelicalism 5. Metuchen, NJ: Scarecrow, 1987.

De La Torre, Miguel A., and Edwin David Aponte. *Introducing Latino/a Theologies*. Maryknoll, NY: Orbis, 2001.

De Leon, Victor. *The Silent Pentecostals: A Biographical History of the Pentecostal Movement among the Hispanics in the Twentieth Century*. La Habra, CA: De Leon, 1979.

Deck, Allan Figueroa. "The Challenge of Evangelical/Pentecostal Christianity to Hispanic Catholicism." In *Hispanic Catholic Culture in the U.S.: Issues and Concerns*, edited by Jay P. Dolan and Allan Figueroa Deck, 461–77. Notre Dame History of Hispanic Catholics in the U.S. 3. Notre Dame: University of Notre Dame Press, 1994.

Del Colle, Ralph. "Spirit-Christology: Dogmatic Foundations for Pentecostal-Charismatic Spirituality." *JPT* 3 (1993) 91–112.

———. *Christ and the Spirit: Spirit-Christology in Trinitarian Perspective*. Oxford: Oxford University Press, 1994.

Dempster, Murray W., Byron D. Klaus, and Douglas Petersen, editors. *The Globalization of Pentecostalism: a Religion Made to Travel*. Irvine, CA: Regnum, 1999.

Depuis, Jacques. *Introducción a la Cristología*. Estella: Editorial Verbo Divino, 1994.

Deschner, John. *Wesley's Christology: An Interpretation*. Dallas: Southern Methodist University Press, 1960.

Domínguez, Roberto. *Pioneros de Pentecostés*. Miami: Literatura Evangélica, 1971.

Doss, Bert H. "A Wonderful Healer—Wonderful Physician." *CGE* 13:9 (1922) 3.

Duffield, Guy P., and Nathaniel M. Van Cleave, editors. *Foundations of Pentecostal Theology.* Los Angeles: L.I.F.E. Bible College, 1983.

Dunn, James D. G. *Baptism in the Holy Spirit: A Re-examination of the New Testament Teaching on the Gift of the Spirit in Relation to Pentecostalism Today.* Philadelphia: Westminster, 1970.

———. *The Christ and the Spirit: Collected Essays of James D. G. Dunn.* 2 vols. Grand Rapids: Eerdmans, 1998.

———. *Christology in the Making: A New Testament Inquiry into the Origins of the Doctrine of the Incarnation.* Philadelphia: Westminster, 1980.

———. *Jesus and the Spirit: A Study of the Religious and Charismatic Experience of Jesus and the First Christians as Reflected in the New Testament.* Philadelphia: Westminster, 1976.

———. "Towards the Spirit of Christ: The Emergence of the Distinctive Features of Christian Pneumatology." In *The Work of the Spirit: Pneumatology and Pentecostalism,* edited by Michael Welker, 3–26. Grand Rapids: Eerdmans, 2006.

Elbert, Paul, editor. *Faces of Renewal: Studies in Honor of Stanley M. Horton Presented on His 70th birthday.* Peabody, MA: Hendrickson, 1988.

Elizondo, Virgilio P. *The Future Is Mestizo: Life Where Cultures Meet.* Oak Park, IL: Meyer-Stone, 1988.

———. *Galilean Journey: The Mexican-American Promise.* Rev. ed. Maryknoll, NY: Orbis, 2000.

Ellacuría, Ignacio. "The Church of the Poor: Historical Sacrament of Liberation," translated by Margaret D. Wilde. In *Mysterium Liberationis: Fundamental Concepts of Liberation Theology,* edited by Ignacio Ellacuría and Jon Sobrino, 543–64. Maryknoll, NY: Orbis, 1993.

———. "The Crucified People," translated by Phillip Berryman and Robert R. Barr. In *Mysterium Liberationis: Fundamental Concepts of Liberation Theology,* edited by Ignacio Ellacuría and Jon Sobrino, 543–64. Maryknoll, NY: Orbis, 1993.

———. *Freedom Made Flesh: The Mission of Christ and His Church.* Translated by John Drury. Maryknoll, NY: Orbis, 1976.

Escobar, Gabriel. "The Complex Tapestry of the Undocumented: Day Laborers Are Just One Strand." Pew Research Center Publications. Online: http://pewresearch.org/pubs/14/the-complex-tapestry-of-the-undocumented.

Espinosa, Gastón. "The Pentecostalization of Latin America and U.S. Latino Christianity." *Pneuma* 26:2 (2004) 262–92.

Espinosa, Gastón, Virgilio Elizondo, and Jesse Miranda, editors. *Latino Religions and Civic Activism in the United States.* Oxford: Oxford University Press, 2005.

Ewart, F. J. "God's Fig Tree Budding." *CGE* 8:28 (1917) 3.

Faupel, David William. *The Everlasting Gospel: The Significance of Eschatology in the Development of Pentecostal Thought.* JPTSup 10. Sheffield: Sheffield Academic, 1996.

Fee, Gordon D. *Pauline Christology: An Exegetical-Theological Study.* Peabody, MA: Hendrickson, 2007.

Frodsham, Stanley H. "Notes from an Eyewitness at the General Council." *The Weekly Evangel* 161 (October 21, 1916) 5.

Gann, Alonzo. "The Manner of Christ's Coming." *CGE* 9:46 (1918) 2.

Gaxiola, Adoniram. "Poverty as a Meeting and Parting Place: Similarities and Contrasts in the Experience of Latin American Pentecostalism and Ecclesial Base Communities." *Pneuma* 13 (1991) 167–74.

Gaxiola-Gaxiola, Manuel J. "Latin American Pentecostalism: A Mosaic within a Mosaic." *Pneuma* 13 (Fall 1991) 107–29.

Gelpi, Donald L. *Pentecostalism: A Theological Viewpoint.* New York: Paulist, 1971.

Gifford, Paul. "The Complex Provenance of Some Elements of African Pentecostal Theology." In *Between Babel and Pentecost: Transnational Pentecostalism in Africa and Latin America*, edited by André Corten and Ruth Marshall-Fratani, 62–79. Indianapolis: Indiana University Press, 2001.

Gill, Kenneth D. *Toward a Contextualized Theology for the Third World: The Emergence and Development of Jesus' Name Pentecostalism in Mexico.* Studies in the Intercultural History of Christianity. Frankfurt: Lang, 1994.

Goizueta, Roberto S. *Caminemos con Jesús: Toward a Hispanic/Latino Theology of Accompaniment.* Maryknoll, NY: Orbis, 1995.

González, Justo L., editor. *Voces: Voices from the Hispanic Church.* Nashville: Abingdon, 1992.

González, Michelle A. "Jesus." In *Handbook of Latina/o Theologies*, edited by Edwin David Aponte and Miguel A. De La Torre, 176–24. St. Louis: Chalice, 2006.

Goodman, M. "The First Jewish Revolt: Social Conflict and the Problem of Debt." *Journal of Jewish Studies* 33 (1982) 418–27.

Gutiérrez, Benjamín F., and Dennis A. Smith, editors. *In the Power of the Spirit. Pentecostals in Latin America: A Challenge to the Historic Churches.* Mexico City: AIPRAL, 1996.

Gutiérrez, Gustavo. *Dios o el Oro de las Indias.* Salamanca: Sígueme, 1990.

———. "Jesús y el Mundo Político." *Perspectivas del Diálogo* 7 (1972) 76–81.

———. *A Theology of Liberation: History, Politics and Salvation.* Translated by Sister Caridad Inda and John Eagleson. Rev. ed. Maryknoll, NY: Orbis, 1988.

Habets, Myk. "Spirit Christology: Seeing in Stereo." *JPT* 11 (2003) 199–234.

Hadsock, Perry, W. "Full Salvation—Its Benefits." *CGE* 11:19 (1920) 4.

Hagnes, Clyde. "Trinity." *CGE* 12:45 (1921) 3.

Haight, Roger. "The Case for Spirit Christology." *Theological Studies* 53 (1992) 257–87.

———. *Jesus, Symbol of God.* Maryknoll, NY: Orbis, 1999.

Hall, J. L. "United Pentecostal Church, International." In *NICPCM*, 1160–65

Hamilton, J. O. "The Trinity in the Godhead." *CGE* 12:30 (1921) 3.

Hanson, K. C., and Douglas E. Oakman. *Palestine in the Time of Jesus: Social Structures and Social Conflicts.* Minneapolis: Fortress, 1998.

Henson, Emma. "Our Coming Lord." *CGE* 8:27 (1917) 3.

Hicks, Eliza. "Jesus the Great Healer." *CGE* 14:31 (1923) 2.

Higgins, John R., Michael L. Dusing, and Frank D. Tallman, editors. *An Introduction to Theology: a Classical Pentecostal Perspective.* Dubuque: Kendall/Hunt, 1994.

Hollenweger, Walter J. "The Pentecostal Elites and the Pentecostal Poor: A Missed Dialogue?" In *Charismatic Christianity as a Global Culture*, edited by Karla Poewe, 200–214. Columbia: University of South Carolina Press, 1994.

———. *Pentecostalism: Origins and Developments Worldwide.* Peabody, MA: Hendrickson, 1997.

Horsley, Richard A. *Sociology and the Jesus Movement*. 2nd ed. New York: Continuum, 1994.

Horton, Stanley M., editor. *Systematic Theology: A Pentecostal Perspective*. Springfield, MO: Logion, 1994.

Hughes, J. P. "New Light a Fallacy." *CGE* 12:35 (1921) 3.

Hunter, Harold D. "The Resurgence of Spirit Christology." *JEPTA* 10:2 (1992) 50–57.

———. *Spirit-Baptism: A Pentecostal Alternative*. New York: University Press of America, 1983.

Hutsell, S. W. "Jesus Is a Great Healer." *CGE* 13:31 (1922) 2.

Hyatt, Eddie L. *The Azusa Street Revival: The Holy Spirit in America: 100 years*. Lake Mary, FL: Charisma/Creation House, 2006.

———. *Fire on the Earth: Eyewitness Reports from the Azusa Street Revival*. Lake Mary, FL: Charisma/Creation House, 2006.

Ingram, Nannie. "Jesus the Great Healer." *CGE* 13:28 (1922) 4.

Ingram, R. J. "Complete Savior." *CGE* 6:26 (1915) 2.

Innes, Stephanie. "Hispanics Fuel Growth in Pentecostal Churches." *The Arizona Republic*, September 2, 2007.

Isasi-Díaz, Ada María. "Christ in *Mujerista* Theology." In *Thinking of Christ: Proclamation, Explanation, Meaning*, edited by Tatha Wiley, 157–76. New York: Continuum, 2003.

Jacobsen, Douglas G. "Knowing the Doctrines of Pentecostals: The Scholastic Theology of the Assemblies of God, 1930–55." In *Pentecostal Currents in American Protestantism*, edited by Edith Blumhofer, Russell Spittler, and Grant Wacker, 90–107. Urbana: University of Illinois Press. 1999.

———. *A Reader in Pentecostal Theology: Voices from the First Generation*. Indianapolis: Indiana University Press, 2006.

———. *Thinking in the Spirit: Theologies of the Early Pentecostal Movement*. Indianapolis: Indiana University Press, 2003.

Jamieson, S. A. "The Trinity." *BM* 256 (June–September 1925) 4.

———. "The Virgin Birth of Our Lord Jesus Christ." *PE* 518 (October 20, 1923) 8–9.

Jenkins, S. D. L. "The Human Son of God and the Holy Spirit: Toward a Pentecostal Incarnational Spirit Christology." PhD diss., Marquette University, 2004.

Johns, Cheryl Bridges. *Pentecostal Formation: A Pedagogy among the Oppressed*. JPTSup 2. Sheffield: Sheffield Academic, 1993.

Johnson, C. W. "Against False Doctrines." *CGE* 11:48 (1920) 4.

Johnston, Robert K. "Pentecostalism and Theological Hermeneutics: Evangelical Options." *Pneuma* 6 (Spring 1984) 51–66.

Kärkkäinen, Veli-Matti. *Christology, a Global Introduction*. Grand Rapids: Baker Academic, 2003.

———. "David's Sling: The Promise and the Problem of Pentecostal Theology Today: A Response to D. Lyle Dabney." *Pneuma* 23 (Spring 2001) 147–52.

———. "Pentecostal Hermeneutics in the Making: On the Way from Fundamentalism to Postmodernism." *JEPTA* 18 (1998) 76–115.

———. *Toward a Pneumatological Theology: Pentecostal and Ecumenical Perspectives on Ecclesiology, Soteriology, and Theology of Mission*. Edited by Amos Yong. Lanham, MD: University Press of America, 2002.

————. *Spiritus ubi vult spirat: Pneumatology in Roman Catholic-Pentecostal Dialogue (1972–1989)*. Schriften der Luther-Agricola-Gesellschaft 42. Helsinki: Luther-Agricolo-Society, 1998.

————. *Ad ultimum terrae: Evangelization, Proselytism and Common Witness in the Roman Catholic-Pentecostal Dialogue (1990–1997)*. Studies in the Intercultural History of Christianity 117. Frankfurt: Lang, 1999.

Kerr, D. W. "The Bible Evidence of the Baptism with the Holy Ghost." *PE* 809 (August 11, 1923) 2.

King, J. H. "From Passover to Pentecost: Chapter XXV from Birth to Baptism, Illustrated in the Life of Jesus." *Pentecostal Holiness Advocate* 11:39 (1928) 9.

————. "He Is the Healer of Every Sickness." *CGE* 11:39 (1920) 3.

Knight, Henry H., III. "From Aldersgate to Azusa: Wesley and the Renewal of Pentecostal Spirituality." *JPT* 8 (April 1996) 82–98.

Küster, Volker, *The Many Faces of Jesus Christ: Intercultural Christology*. Maryknoll, NY: Orbis, 2001.

Lampe, Geoffrey W. H. *God as Spirit*. Bampton Lectures, 1976. Oxford: Clarendon, 1977.

Land, Steven J. *Pentecostal Spirituality: A Passion for the Kingdom*. JPTSup 1. Sheffield: Sheffield Academic, 1993.

Langford, Thomas A. "John Wesley and Theological Method." In *Rethinking Wesley's Theology for Contemporary Methodism*, edited by Randy L. Maddox, 35–48. Nashville: Abingdon, 1998.

Lawrence, B. Freeman. "Jesus Christ Our Theme." *The Pentecost* 2:9 (1910) 1.

Lee, F. J. "Three in One." *CGE* 12:38 (1921) 3.

————. "The Trinity Finally in One." *CGE* 13:36 (1922) 3.

Lewis, Paul W. "Reflections on a Hundred Years of Pentecostal Theology." *Cyberjournal for Pentecostal-Charismatic Research* 12 (February 2003). Online: http://www .pctii.org/cyberj/cyberj12/lewis.html.

Lingerfelt, P. R. "Jesus Her Only Physician." *CGE* 12:21 (1921) 4.

Llewellyn, J. S. "Distinction in the Godhead." *CGE* 14:21 (1923) 1.

Loewe, William P. "Two Revisionist Christologies of Presence: Roger Haight and Piet Schoonenberg." In *A Sacramental Life: A Festschrift Honoring Bernard Cooke*, edited by Michael Horace Barnes and William P. Roberts, 93–116. Marquette Studies in Theology 37. Milwaukee: Marquette University Press, 2003.

Lois, Julio. "Christology in the Theology of Liberation," transalated by Robert R. Barr. In *Mysterium Liberationis: Fundamental Concepts of Liberation Theology*, edited by Ignacio Ellacuría and Jon Sobrino, 168–94. Maryknoll, NY: Orbis, 1993.

López R., Darío. *La Mision Liberadora de Jesus: El Mensaje del Evangelio de Lucas*. Ediciones Puma; CENIP, 2004.

"The Lord for the Body." *BM* 273 (July–September 1929) 10.

Lucas, Isidro. *The Browning of America: The Hispanic Revolution in the American Church*. Chicago: Fides/Claretian, 1981.

Ma, Wonsuk, and Robert P. Menzies, editors. *The Spirit and Spirituality: Essays in Honour of Russell P. Spittler*. JPTSup 24. Edinburg: T. & T. Clark, 2004.

Macchia, Frank D. *Baptized in the Spirit: A Global Pentecostal Theology*. Grand Rapids: Zondervan, 2006.

————. "Theology." In *NIDPCM*, 1120–41.

Mackay, John A. *The Other Spanish Christ: A Study in the Spiritual History of Spain and South America.* New York: Macmillan, 1933.

Maddox, Randy L. *Responsible Grace: John Wesley's Practical Theology.* Nashville: Abingdon, 1994.

Malone, Edna. "There Is Power in the Blood of Jesus." *CGE* 16:8 (1925) 4.

Mariz, Cecília Loreto. *Coping with Poverty: Pentecostals and Christian Base Communities in Brazil.* Philadelphia: Temple University Press, 1994.

Martin, David. *Pentecostalism: The World Their Parish.* Religion and Modernity. Malden, MA: Blackwell, 2002.

McGee, Gary B. "All for Jesus: The Revival Legacy of A.B. Simpson." In *Enrichment Journal: A Journal for Pentecostal Ministry* 4:3 (1999) 82. Online: http://www.ag.org/enrichmentjournal/199902/ 082_all_for_jesus.cfm.

———. "Historical Background." In *Systematic Theology*, edited by Stanley M. Horton. Springfield. Logion, 1994.

McPherson, Aimee Semple. "Holy Spirit." *The Bridal Call* 7:2 (1923) 4.

McRoberts, Kerry D. "The Holy Trinity." In *Systematic Theology: A Pentecostal Perspective*, edited by Stanley M. Horton, 145–77. Springfield, MO: Logion, 1994.

Meier, John P. *A Marginal Jew: Rethinking the Historical Jesus.* Vol 1: *The Roots of the Problem and the Person.* New York: Doubleday, 1991.

Mejido, Manuel Jesús. "U.S. Hispanics/Latinos and the Field of Graduate Theological Education." *Theological Education* 34:2 (1998) 51–72

Menzies, Robert P. *Empowered for Witness: The Spirit in Luke-Acts.* JPTSup 6. Sheffield: Sheffield Academic, 1994.

Menzies, William W. *Bible Doctrines: A Pentecostal Perspective.* Springfield, MO: Logion, 1993.

Menzies, William W., and Robert P. Menzies. "Healing in the Atonement." In *Spirit and Power: Foundation of Pentecostal Experience: A Call to Evangelical Dialogue.* Grand Rapids: Zondervan, 2000.

Migliore, Daniel L. "Christology in Context: The Doctrinal and Contextual Tasks of Christology Today." *Interpretation* 49 (1995) 242–54.

Míguez Bonino, José. *Faces of Latin American Protestantism: 1993 Carnahan Lectures.* Translated by Eugene L. Stockwell. Grand Rapids: Eerdmans, 1997.

Míguez Bonino, José, Juan Sepúlveda, and Rigoberto Gálvez, editors. *Unidad y Diversidad del Protestantismo Latinoamericano: El Testimonio Evangélico Hacia el Tercer Milenio: Palabra, Espíritu y Misión.* Buenos Aires: Kairos Ediciones, 2002.

Miranda, Andrés, editor. "Jesús, el Verbo Hecho Carne." *El Maestro Pentecostés* 58:31 (2002–2003) 131–38.

Miranda, Jesse, and E. L. Wilson. "Hispanic Pentecostalism." In *NIDPCM*, 715–23.

Mittelstadt, Martin William. "Christology." In *Encyclopedia of Pentecostal and Charismatic Christianity*, edited by Stanley M. Burgess, 97–100. New York: Routledge, 2006.

Mobley, Nancy. "The Lord Is Her Healer." *CGE* 12:14 (1921) 4.

Nelson, P. C. *Bible Doctrines; A Series of Studies Based on the Statement of Fundamental Truths as Adopted by the Assemblies of God.* Springfield, MO: Gospel, 1971.

———. "Deliverance to the Captives." *PE* 705 (July 9, 1927) 6–7.

Newman, Paul W. *A Spirit Christology: Recovering the Biblical Paradigm of Christian Faith*. New York: University Press of America, 1987.

Nichols, David R. "The Lord Jesus Christ." In *Systematic Theology: A Pentecostal Perspective*, edited by Stanley M. Horton, 291–324. Rev. ed. Springfield, MO: Logion, 1995.

Norris, Richard A., Jr., editor and translator. *The Christological Controversy*. Sources of Early Christian Thought. Philadelphia: Fortress, 1980.

Nuñez, Emilio A. *Liberation Theology*. Translated by Paul E. Sywulka. Chicago: Moody, 1985.

O'Keefe, Michael E. "The Spirit Christology of Piet Schoonenberg." In *Christology: Memory, Inquiry, Practice*, edited by Anne M. Clifford and Anthony J. Godzieba, 116–40. Annual Publication of the College Theology 48 (2002). Maryknoll, NY: Orbis, 2003.

O'neal, Richard. "Power in the Blood." *CGE* 11:51 (1920) 3.

Orwig, A. W. "Jesus as Saviour and Healer." *BM* 3:55 (1910) 1.

Padilla, C. René. "Toward a Contextual Christology from Latin America." In *Conflict and Context: Hermeneutics in the Americas*, edited by Mark Lau Branson and C. René Padilla, 81–91. Grand Rapids: Eerdmans, 1986.

Padilla, Elaine. "Pentecostal Theology." In *Encyclopedia of Pentecostal and Charismatic Christianity*, edited by Stanley M. Burgess, 355–59. New York: Routledge, 2006.

Pardington, G. P. *Twenty-Five Wonderful Years, 1889–1914: A Popular Sketch of the Christian and Missionary Alliance*. New York: Christian Alliance, 1914.

Pearlman, Myer. *Knowing the Doctrines of the Bible*. Springfield, MO: Gospel, 1937.

Pecota, Daniel B. "The Saving Work of Christ." In *Systematic Theology: A Pentecostal Perspective*, edited by Stanley M. Horton, 325–73. Springfield, MO: Logion, 1994.

Pedraja, Luis G. "Doing Christology in Spanish." *Theology Today* 54:4 (1998) 453–63.

———. *Jesus Is My Uncle: Christology from a Hispanic Perspective*. Nashville: Abingdon, 1999.

Perry, Sam C. "The Blood of Jesus." *CGE* 5:12 (1914) 6.

———. "A Bloodless Salvation?" *CGE* 6:25 (1915) 3.

———. "Christ Our Healer and Health." *CGE* 5:13 (1914) 6.

———. "Jesus Is Coming." *CGE* 5:39 (1914) 6.

Peterson, Douglas. *Not by Might, Nor by Power: A Pentecostal Theology of Social Concern in Latin America*. Regnum: Oxford, 1996.

Pew Hispanic Center. "Statistical Portrait of Hispanics in the United States, 2006." January 2008. Online: http://pewhispanic.org/factsheets/factsheet.php?Fact sheetID=35.

Phan, Peter C. *Christianity with an Asian Face: Asian American Theology in the Making*. Maryknoll, NY: Orbis, 2003.

Pinnock, Clark H. "Divine Relationality: A Pentecostal Contribution to the Doctrine of God." *JPT* 16 (2000) 3–26.

———. *Flame of Love: A Theology of the Holy Spirit*. Downers Grove, IL: InterVarsity, 1996.

Pope-Levison, Priscilla, and John R. Levison. *Jesus in Global Contexts*. Louisville: Westminster John Knox, 1992.

Porterfield, Amanda. *Healing in the History of Christianity*. Oxford: Oxford University Press, 2005.

Purves, Jim. "The Interaction of Christology and Pneumatology in the Soteriology of Edward Irving." *Pneuma* 14 (Spring 1992) 81–90.

Ramirez, Daniel. "Alabaré a mi Señor: Hymnody as Ideology in Latino Protestantism." In *Singing the Lord's Song in a Strange Land: Hymnody in the History of North American Protestantism*, edited by Edith L. Blumhofer and Mark A. Noll, 196–218. Religion and American Culture. Tuscaloosa: University of Alabama Press, 2004.

————. "Public Lives in American Hispanic Churches: Expanding the Paradigm." In *Latino Religions and Civic Activism in the United States*, edited by Gastón Espinosa, Virgilio Elizondo, and Jesse Miranda, 177–95. Oxford: Oxford University Press, 2005.

Ramos, Rigoberto. "La Sencillez de la Encarnación." *El Evangelio* 54:4 (1999) 8–9.

Ray, L. A. "Victory through the Blood of Jesus." *CGE* 11:27 (1920) 3.

Reed, D. A. "Oneness Pentecostalism." In *The International Dictionary of Pentecostal and Charismatic Movements*, edited by Stanley M. Burgess and Eduard M. Van Der Maas, 936–44. Grand Rapids: Zondervan.

Recinos, Harold J. *Good News from the Barrio: Prophetic Witness for the Church.* Louisville: Westminster John Knox, 2006.

Rivera, Roberto A., editor. "El Dios Encarnado." *El Maestro Pentecostés* 54:23 (1998–1999) 5–11.

Rivera Pagán, Luis N. *A Violent Evangelism: The Political and Religious Conquest of the Americas.* Louisville: Westminster John Knox, 1992.

Rollins, F. W. "Composed of Three." *CGE* 17:1 (1926) 4.

Roth, S. John. *The Blind, the Lame, and the Poor: Character Types in Luke-Acts.* JSNTSup 144. Sheffield: Sheffield Academic, 1997.

Ruthven, Jon. M. "Jesus as Rabbi: A Mimesis Christology: The Charismatic Pattern of Discipleship in the New Testament." Society of Pentecostal Studies Annual Papers 1. 1998. Online: http://faithstreamhost.net/pentecostalministers/ dmdoc uments/Jesus%20as%20Rabbi-A%20Mimesis%20Christology%20-%20The%20 Charismatic%20Pattern%20of%20Discipleship%20in%20the%20New%20 Testament.htm.

Rybarczyk, Edmund J. *Beyond Salvation: Eastern Orthodoxy and Classical Pentecostalism on Becoming Like Christ.* Paternoster Theological Monographs. Carlisle, UK: Paternoster, 2004.

Salter, James. "God's Man in the Holy Ghost." *The Latter Rain Evangel* 18:3 (1925) 4–7.

Sánchez-Walsh, Arlene M. *Latino Pentecostal Identity: Evangelical Faith, Self, and Society.* New York: Columbia University Press, 2003.

Sanders, Cheryll Jeanne. *Saints in Exile: The Holiness-Pentecostal Experience in African American Religion and Culture.* New York: Oxford University Press, 1996.

Santos, Wilfredo Nieves. "La Verdad de la Navidad." *El Evangelio* 53:4 (1998) 27.

Schoonenberg, Piet. *El Espíritu, la Palabra y el Hijo.* Translated by Ramon Puig Massana from the German, *Der Geist, das Wort und der Sohn.* Salamanca: Sígueme, 1998.

————. "Spirit Christology and Logos Christology." *Bijdragen* 38 (1977) 350–75.

Seccombe, David Peter. *Possessions and the Poor in Luke-Acts.* Studien zum Neuen Testament und seiner Umwelt, series B, 6. Linz: Fuchs, 1983.

Segundo, Juan Luis. *Jesus of Nazareth, Yesterday and Today.* Vol. 2: *The Historical Jesus of the Synoptics.* Translated by John Drury. Maryknoll, NY: Orbis, 1985.

Sexton, E. A. "Divine Healing: Jesus Our Healer." *BM* 2:35 (1909) 1.

Seymour, William J. "Back to Pentecost." *AF* 1:2 (1906) 3.

———. "The Baptism of the Holy Ghost." *AF* 2:13 (1908) 3.

———. "Christ's Messages to the Church." *AF* 1:11 (1908) 2.

———. "The Holy Ghost and the Bride." *AF* 2:13 (1908) 4.

———. "Jesus' First Sermon after His Baptism." *AF* 2:13 (1908) 3.

———. "Our Lord's Finished Work." *BM* 5:104 (1912) 1.

———. "The Pentecostal Baptism Restored." *AF* 1:2 (1906) 1.

———. "The Precious Atonement." *AF* 1:1 (1906) 2.

———. "Rebecca: Type of the Bride of Christ—Gen. 24." *AF* 1:6 (1907) 2.

———. "Salvation and Healing." *AF* 1:4 (1906) 2.

———. "Sanctified on the Cross." *AF* 2:13 (1908) 2.

———. "The Spotless Lamb of God." *AF* 1:4 (1906) 4.

———. Untitled article. *AF* 1:10 (1907) 3.

———. "Virtue in the Perfect Body of Jesus." *AF* 1:6 (1907) 2.

———. "The Way into the Holiest." *AF* 1:2 (1906) 4.

Shaull, Richard, and Waldo Cesar. *Pentecostalism and the Future of Christian Churches: Promises, Limitations, Challenges.* Grand Rapids: Eerdmans, 2000.

Shepherd, B. L. "The Lord Still Performs Miracles." *CGE* 11:5 (1920) 4.

Shepherd of Hermas. Edited and translated by Bart D. Ehrman. Loeb Classical Library 2. Cambridge: Harvard University Press, 2003.

———. Translated by Kirsopp Lake. Loeb Classical Library 2. Cambridge: Harvard University Press, 1919.

Simpson, A. B. *The Four-Fold Gospel.* New York: Gospel Alliance, 1925.

———. *The Holy Spirit, or, Power from on High: An Unfolding of the Doctrine of the Holy Spirit in the Old and New Testaments.* Vol. 2. Harrisburg, PA: Christian, 1895.

———. *Walking in the Spirit.* Harrisburg, PA: Christian Pub., 1895.

Simpson, W. W. "The Glory Given. John 17:32." *The Weekly Evangel* 228 (February 23, 1918) 2.

Slaaté, Howard A. *A Purview of Wesley's Theology.* New York: University Press of America, 2000.

Sobrino, Jon. *Christ the Liberator: A View from the Victims.* Translated by Paul Burns. Maryknoll, NY: Orbis, 2001.

———. *Christology at the Crossroads: A Latin American Approach.* Translated by John Drury. Maryknoll, NY: Orbis, 1978.

———. *Jesus in Latin America.* Maryknoll, NY: Orbis, 1987.

———. *Jesus the Liberator: A Historical-Theological Reading of Jesus of Nazareth.* Translated by Paul Burns and Francis McDonagh. Maryknoll, NY: Orbis, 1993.

———. "Systematic Christology: Jesus Christ, the Absolute Mediator of the Reign of God," translated by Robert R. Barr. In *Mysterium Liberationis: Fundamental Concepts of Liberation Theology,* edited by Ignacio Ellacuría and Jon Sobrino, 440–61. Maryknoll, NY: Orbis, 1993.

Solivan, Samuel. *The Spirit, Pathos and Liberation: Toward an Hispanic Pentecostal Theology.* JPTSup 14. Sheffield: Sheffield Academic, 1998.